Built to Bend

How to Adapt, Protect, and Grow Your Money When Life Changes

Sekhar Burra

Dedicated to my mother

Contents

Preface · Why I Wrote Built to Bend

Most people are not financially vulnerable because they lack ambition. They are vulnerable because their financial life has quietly become too rigid.

Their income depends on a single job. Their lifestyle depends on everything continuing to go right. Their expenses are hard to bring down. Their debt payments leave almost no breathing room. Their investments are built for growth but not for uncertainty. And their biggest money decisions are too often made under pressure in a hurry, in fear, or in comparison to someone else.

For a while, a life like that can look like success. The house is nice. The car is nice. The career looks stable. The vacations happen, the retirement account grows, the bills get paid on time.

Then something changes.

A job is lost. Business slows. A parent gets sick. Interest rates climb. Inflation pushes up the cost of an ordinary month. Markets fall at the exact moment cash is needed. A child needs help. A marriage changes shape. A new technology rewrites the value of a skill that took years to build. Or just as often an opportunity appears, and there is simply no room to reach for it.

In those moments, people discover a truth that was never printed on the brochure: **financial success is not only about how much money you make. It is about how much room your money gives you to move.**

That idea is the reason this book exists.

For decades, the formula was simple, and it carried real wisdom: study hard, find a steady job, buy a home, save consistently, invest in retirement, and things will work out. The problem is not that the formula was wrong. It is that, for most people now, life no longer travels in a straight line. The ground keeps shifting underneath us and a comfortable household can suddenly feel stretched, not because anyone was careless, but because the environment changed around them.

This is why financial agility matters.

Financial agility is the ability to adapt when financial conditions change. It is not about being rich, and it is not only about budgeting or investing. It is the ability to protect yourself through a shock, make sound decisions under pressure, and be positioned to act when an opportunity finally arrives.

A financially agile person asks better questions than *"How much money do I have?"* They ask:

How long could I last if my income stopped tomorrow? How quickly could I bring my expenses down? How dependent am I on one job, one client, one skill, one market? Will I have cash when others are forced to sell? Could my family adjust without panic? Am I building options or building a life that breaks the moment it is tested?

This is the difference between optimization and adaptation, and it runs through the whole book. Traditional personal finance is mostly about optimization squeezing out the best result when things go as expected. Agility is about what happens when they don't.

Optimization asks, *"How do I get the highest return?"* Agility asks, *"Will I still be okay if my assumptions are wrong?"*

Optimization asks, *"Can I afford this payment?"* Agility asks, *"Can I still afford it if my income drops, my costs rise, or rates move against me?"*

Optimization asks, *"What is the best plan?"* Agility asks, *"How do I build a life that can survive more than one plan?"*

So let me be clear about what you are holding.

This is **not** a book about getting rich quickly. It is not a book about extreme frugality or punishing yourself into wealth. It is not a book about predicting markets, timing the economy, or following one perfect formula because the entire premise here is that the formula will eventually meet a reality it did not expect.

This **is** a book about building a financial life that can bend without breaking one that can adapt, protect, and grow. To adapt is to adjust when conditions change. To protect is to absorb a setback and recover your footing afterward. To grow is to use a steady foundation to reach for something better. A financial life with those three capacities is not fragile. It is not trapped by every bill, every payment, every paycheck, every surprise. It has breathing room. It has choices. It has protection. It has direction.

It is, in the end, a financial operating system for uncertain times.

You do not need to be wealthy to begin. This book is for professionals and families, for entrepreneurs and freelancers for anyone who wants a more flexible, more resilient relationship with money. What it asks of you is not a bigger income or a perfect forecast. It asks for awareness, a simple system, better decisions, and a little courage: the willingness to redesign parts of your financial life *before* life forces the redesign on you.

The goal is not to predict the future. No one can, and you do not need to. The goal is to become harder to break and better prepared to act to build a money life that does not freeze when everything around it is changing.

Because life will bend you. The question this book answers is how to bend with it, and come back stronger instead of breaking.

Part One · Why a Financial Life Must Bend

The tallest skyscrapers are designed to sway. On a windy day, the top of a thousand-foot tower can move several feet from center, and the engineers who built it consider that a success. A structure that refused to move at all that met every gust with total rigidity wouldn't be stronger. It would crack. The same is true of bridges, of aircraft wings, of the tallest trees in a storm. The things that last are not the ones that resist force. They're the ones built to bend.

Most of us were handed a financial plan built to do the opposite.

The deal sounded reasonable: get a good education, land a steady job, buy a house, save a little every month, invest for the long run, and arrive at a comfortable retirement. It was a straight line from here to there, and for a long time, for a lot of people, the line mostly held. So we organized our money around the assumption that it would keep holding that income would rise steadily, that careers would last decades, that the cost of a home and an education and a normal life would stay within reach.

Then the line stopped being straight.

Careers now get interrupted by layoffs, restructurings, and technologies that rewrite whole professions in a few years. Prices surge and ease in ways that no household budget was designed to absorb. Interest rates move, and with them the cost of every dollar you owe. People change cities, change partners, change fields, support aging parents and growing kids at the same time, and live longer than any retirement math assumed. None of this means the old advice was wrong. Saving still matters. Investing still works. But the advice was *incomplete*, because it prepared you for a life that went according to plan and almost no life does.

Here is the uncomfortable thing this part of the book asks you to sit with: the reason so many people feel financially fragile is not, mostly, that they failed to save enough. It's that their money can't move. Income is tied to a single employer. Expenses are locked in at the very top of what they earn. Debt payments leave no slack. Everything is technically *fine* as long as nothing changes. And then something changes, because something always does, and a life that looked stable turns out to have been merely stiff.

Stability and agility are not the same thing. Stability is being okay when conditions hold. Agility is being okay when they don't. This book is about the second kind, because the second kind is the only one life actually lets you keep.

Before we touch a single tactic before budgets, buffers, debt, or investing we need to look honestly at why a financial life has to bend in the first place. That's the work of Part One. In **Chapter 1**, we'll look at what really broke in the straight-line money life, and why "responding to change" has quietly become the most valuable financial skill there is. In **Chapter 2**, we'll go hunting for rigidity in your own finances the hidden places where your money has lost the ability to move. In **Chapter 3**, you'll learn to read the four kinds of weather every financial life passes through, so you stop being surprised by the storms. And in **Chapter 4**, before anyone tells you what to do, you'll decide what you stand for a short set of money values and principles that will make every hard decision in the rest of the book easier.

None of this is about predicting the future. You can't, and you don't need to. It's about building a financial life with enough give that the future doesn't get to break it.

Let's start with what changed.

Chapter 1 · The End of the Straight-Line Money Life

There was a plan, and for a long time it worked.

You probably know it by heart, because some version of it was handed to nearly everyone. Study hard. Earn a credential. Find a good job and hold onto it. Buy a home as early as you can. Save a steady slice of every paycheck, invest it for the long run, and one day retire with enough to be comfortable. It was less a strategy than a story a straight line drawn from your first day of work to your last, each step leading cleanly into the next. Follow the line, the story promised, and you would be fine.

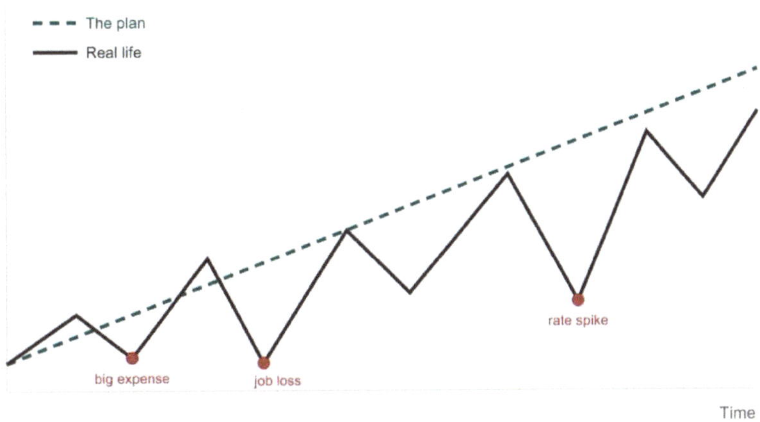

The plan assumes a straight line; a real financial life zigzags.

For a few decades, across much of North America and almost everywhere else in the world, the line mostly held. And it's worth being honest about *why* it held, because the advice wasn't foolish. It fit the world that produced it. People often spent decades at a single employer, and that employer frequently funded their retirement directly. A home was something an ordinary income could reach, and its value tended to climb. The cost of an education and the cost of a normal middle-class life stayed within a recognizable relationship to wages. Inflation was, for long stretches, mild and predictable. In a world that stable, planning in a straight line was a reasonable thing to do, because the ground under the line stayed roughly where you left it.

That world has not vanished entirely. Saving still works. Investing still compounds. Owning a home is still, for many people, a fine decision. The wisdom in the old advice is real, and this book is not going to tell you to throw it away. But the world that made the straight line *reliable* has quietly come apart, and most of us are still planning as though it hasn't.

What bent the line

Five forces, working together, turned a dependable straight line into something far less certain. None of them is a secret. What's easy to miss is how completely they've changed the kind of planning that actually keeps a person safe.

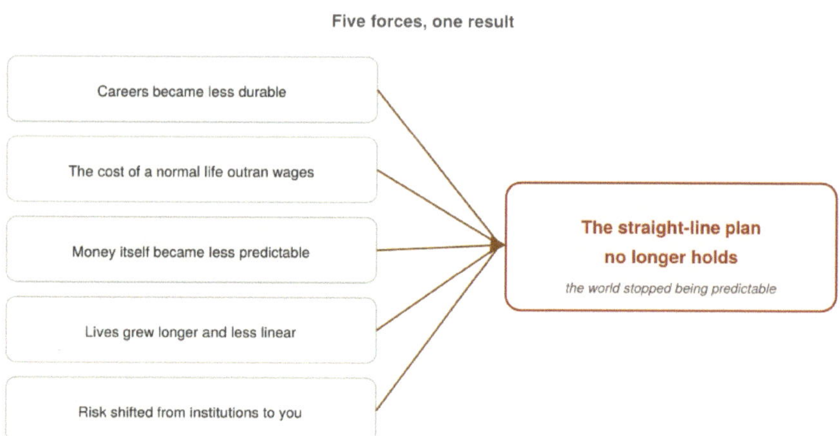

Five forces press on the old straight-line plan at once.

The first is that **careers stopped being durable.** The idea of joining a company and rising through it until retirement now describes a shrinking minority of working lives. Industries get disrupted in years rather than generations. Roles are automated, reorganized, offshored, or simply dissolved. Whole categories of work appear and disappear inside a single career, and the most recent wave software that can do slices of knowledge work is reshaping professions that felt untouchable a decade ago. The practical effect is that your income, the engine of the entire plan, sits on ground that can shift without warning.

The second is that **the cost of a normal life outran wages.** In many cities, the price of a home has climbed far faster than the income needed to buy one, so the "just buy a house" step that once anchored the plan has become, for a lot of people, the step they can't take or can only take by stretching themselves to the edge. Education, childcare, and healthcare have followed similar curves. The arithmetic that worked for an earlier generation, where a single ordinary income could carry a household and still leave room to save, no longer adds up the same way.

The third is that **money itself became less predictable.** Interest rates can sit near zero for years and then climb sharply, changing the cost of every dollar you owe almost overnight. Inflation can stay quiet for a generation and then return, quietly eroding the value of the savings you worked hard to build. These aren't abstractions. They decide whether your mortgage payment is comfortable or crushing, whether your cash cushion holds its value or shrinks while it sits.

The fourth is that **lives got longer and far less linear.** People live longer, which means retirements to fund that can stretch thirty years or more a length the old math never assumed. And the path there rarely runs straight anymore. Careers pause for caregiving. People change fields in their forties, start over in their fifties, raise children later, support aging parents and growing kids in the same stretch of years. A plan built for one continuous arc strains against a life that bends in several directions.

The fifth force ties the others together: **risk has shifted from institutions onto individuals.** A generation ago, large parts of financial uncertainty were absorbed by employers and governments. Pensions promised a defined outcome; the institution carried the investment risk. Steady employment spread the risk of a bad year. Today, much of that risk has been handed to you. Retirement now usually means a self-directed account whose performance is your problem. Stable employment has given way, for many, to contract and gig arrangements where the cushion between you and a bad month is whatever you built yourself. You are now the one carrying job risk, investment risk, and longevity risk often without anyone telling you the handoff occurred.

The quiet danger of a brittle plan

Here is the part that catches people off guard. A plan built for a straight line doesn't just become *less useful* when the line bends. It becomes a source of false safety.

A detailed plan feels like protection. You can see the numbers, the projections, the tidy upward curve. But a plan that assumes continuity steady income, stable costs, predictable returns is only as strong as that assumption, and the assumption is exactly the thing the modern world keeps breaking. The plan looks robust right up until the moment reality diverges from it, and then it offers almost nothing, because it was never designed to handle the divergence. It was designed to be *followed*, not *changed.*

This is the trap. The danger isn't having a plan. The danger is having *only* a plan a single forecast you've quietly bet your security on, with no built-in capacity to revise it when the facts move. The more detailed and confident the plan is, the more dangerous this can be, because precision feels like safety even when it's resting on assumptions that no longer hold.

Responding to change over following the plan

So what replaces the straight line?

Not a better straight line. Not a more detailed forecast, not a cleverer projection, not a plan so airtight that nothing can disturb it no such plan exists. What replaces it is a different skill entirely, and it's the first idea this whole book is built on: **responding to change over following the plan.**

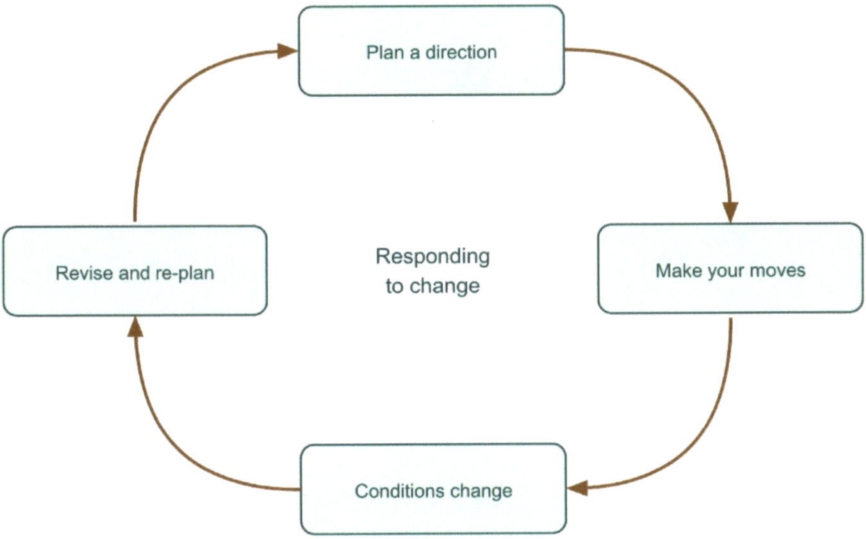

Responding to change is a cycle, not a one-time plan.

The phrase is borrowed, deliberately. Decades ago, the people building software ran into the same wall in their own work. They had been taught to plan a project completely up front and then execute the plan exactly, and they kept watching those plans shatter on contact with reality requirements changed, markets moved, the thing they'd carefully specified a year ago was no longer the thing anyone needed. The breakthrough wasn't a better up-front plan. It was a shift in what they valued: the team that could *adapt* reliably beat the team with the most detailed forecast. They still planned. They simply stopped treating the plan as a promise and started treating it as a current best guess, to be revised the moment better information arrived.

Apply that to money and almost everything changes. You still plan you still set goals, still project, still decide on a direction. But you hold the plan loosely, and you build your financial life so that changing it doesn't require a crisis. The measure of a good financial plan stops being *how detailed is it?* and becomes *how well can it absorb being wrong?* Because it will be wrong. Some assumption inside it about your income, your costs, the economy, your own life will eventually turn out not to hold. The question is whether that discovery is a manageable adjustment or a catastrophe.

That single shift, from following to responding, is what separates a financial life that breaks under pressure from one that bends.

The same shock, two different lives

Picture two people, both good earners, both hit by the same kind of event: their industry shifts, and the role each has held for years disappears.

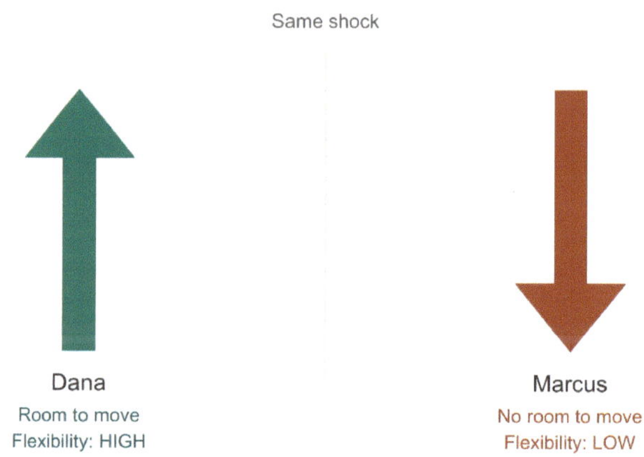

Same shock, two outcomes the difference is built in advance.

The first, call her Dana, had spent the prior years doing something that looked, from the outside, almost boring. She kept her skills current even when her job didn't demand it. She kept her fixed costs comfortably below what she earned, so her lifestyle never climbed to the very top of her income. She kept several months of spending in accessible cash. When her division was cut, it was genuinely hard the loss was real, the fear was real. But she had *room*. She could take a contract role at lower pay for a while without panic, because her costs could shrink to meet the smaller income. She could spend a few months retraining into an adjacent field, because the cash cushion bought her that time. Within a year she had changed direction, and the change, while painful, didn't threaten the foundation of her life. Her plan had been wrong about the future, and it didn't matter much, because the plan could change.

The second, call him Marcus, earned more than Dana noticeably more. And he had done what the straight line told him to do, optimized for it, in fact. He'd bought the largest home the bank would approve, with a payment sized to his income at its peak. The cars, the children's activities, the lifestyle had all risen to match what he made. His savings were real but locked away in long-term, hard-to-reach places, because that's where the projections said they'd grow best. His sense of who he was had grown into the role itself. When the same kind of shock hit him, the difference wasn't his income. It was that he had no room to move. The big payment didn't shrink just because his paycheck did. The lifestyle couldn't contract quickly without a painful unwinding. The savings weren't available without a penalty. Every part of his financial life had been tuned for the plan to continue and when it didn't, there was no give anywhere. The same event that bent Dana's life nearly broke his.

The lesson isn't that Marcus should have earned less or enjoyed his life less. It's that earning more had hidden how stuck he'd become. His finances were optimized and fragile at the same time, and he couldn't see it, because as long as the line stayed straight, everything looked like success.

What this book is really building toward

If there's one idea to carry out of this chapter, it's this: the goal is not to draw a better straight line. The goal is to build a financial life that can change direction.

That's a different project than the one most of us were handed. It's less about predicting the right future and more about being able to handle several. It's less about the perfect plan and more about the room to revise it. It asks a question the old advice never did not just *will this work if everything goes as expected?* but *will I still be okay if it doesn't?*

The rest of this book is the answer to that question, built one piece at a time. But before we can construct anything, we have to look honestly at where you've already lost the ability to move the places your financial life has quietly stiffened without your noticing. That's where we go next.

Chapter summary:

- The traditional path educate, work, buy, save, retire carried real wisdom, but it quietly assumed a continuity the world no longer provides.
- Five forces bent the straight line: careers stopped being durable, the cost of a normal life outran wages, money itself became less predictable, lives grew longer and less linear, and financial risk shifted from institutions onto individuals.

- A plan built for a straight line offers false safety; the danger isn't having a plan, it's having only a plan, with no built-in capacity to revise it.
- The skill that replaces the straight line is responding to change over following the plan you still plan, but you hold it loosely and build enough room that changing course doesn't require a crisis.

Questions to think about:

- Think of the last three unexpected money events in your life. For each one, did your plan flex, or did it break?
- How much of your current financial plan quietly assumes that things will stay roughly as they are today?
- If your role or industry changed within the next two years, how quickly could your finances change with it?
- Where might you, like Marcus, be optimized and fragile at the same time looking successful while quietly losing room to move?

Chapter 2 · When Money Gets Stuck

You almost certainly know someone who looks successful and feels trapped.

The job is good. The house is nice, the car is newer than yours, the vacations actually happen. From the outside, the picture is exactly what the straight line promised. But underneath it runs a quiet, constant tension, because they sense even if they never say it that none of it could survive a real disruption. A missed bonus, a few months without the paycheck, and the whole structure would start to wobble. By the numbers, they are doing fine. They are also completely stuck.

This is one of the most common and least discussed conditions in personal finance, and it has almost nothing to do with how much a person earns. We're taught to equate financial trouble with not having enough. But there is a second kind of trouble, harder to see and, in a changing world, often more dangerous: having plenty and being unable to move it. There isn't a tidy word for it, so I'll use a plain one. Let's call it being *stuck*.

The comfortable trap

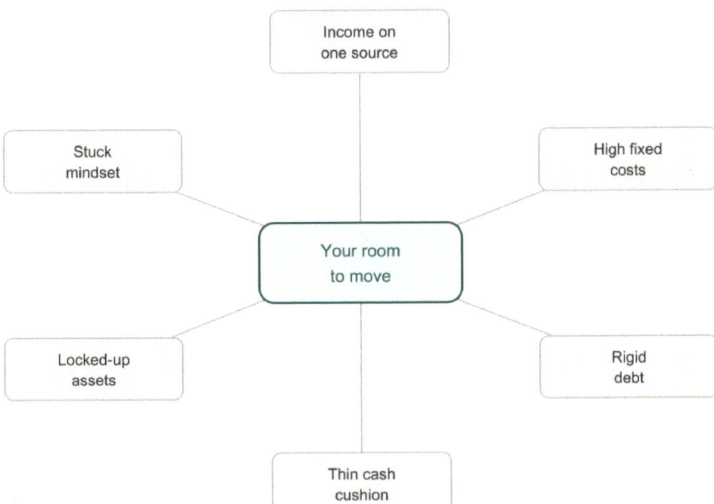

Rigidity isn't one problem; it hides in six places.

Here is how it usually happens, and notice that nothing in the story is reckless. A person earns more over time, which is exactly what they were supposed to do. And as the income rose, the life rose with it. A bigger home, because they could finally afford one. A better car, with a payment to match. Children's activities, a certain standard of vacation, the small monthly subscriptions that each seem trivial. None of it was extravagant in the moment. But step by step, the obligations expanded until the space between what comes in and what must go out had nearly closed. As income increased, expenses adjusted to match it, quietly keeping the comfortable trap intact.

The salary that was supposed to buy freedom had quietly purchased a set of commitments that now *require* the salary. This is what people mean by golden handcuffs, though the handcuffs aren't really the job they're the fixed shape of the life the job pays for. And as we saw in the last chapter, a life that only works as long as nothing changes is living on borrowed time, because something always changes.

The six places money gets stuck

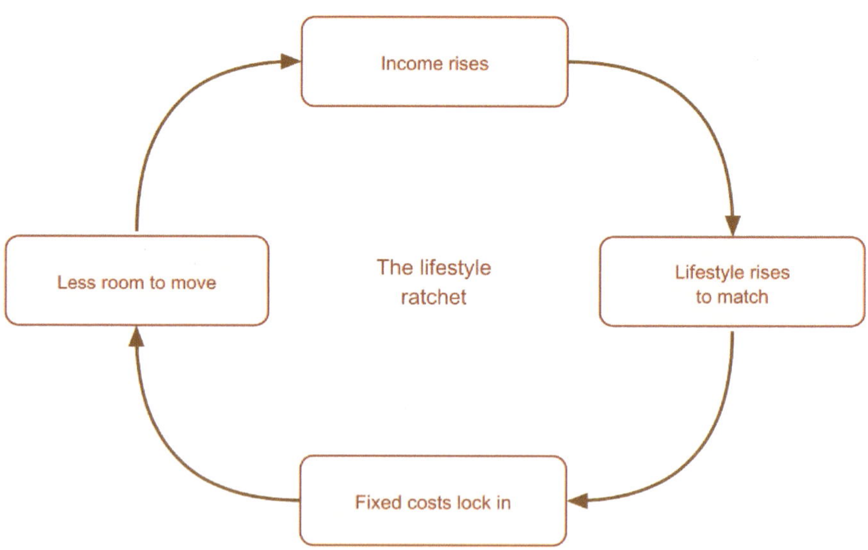

The lifestyle ratchet: each raise quietly becomes the new normal.

Rigidity is rarely one big, obvious problem. It hides, and it hides in six fairly predictable places. Learning to see all six is the first step to loosening any of them.

The first is **income concentration.** When your income comes from a single source one employer, one major client, one narrow skill, one industry your entire financial life rests on a single point of failure. It feels stable right up until that one source falters, and then everything falters at once.

The second is **high fixed costs.** Some expenses flex easily; others are locked in by contract or habit the large mortgage or rent, the car payments, the commitments that don't shrink just because your income did. The higher your fixed costs sit as a share of what you earn, the less shock your finances can absorb before something has to give.

The third is **rigid debt.** Not all debt is equal. Debt that carries a large, unavoidable monthly payment, or that can swing with interest rates, removes room to move at exactly the moments you need it most. It commits your future income before that income has even arrived.

The fourth is **a thin cash cushion.** When almost everything you have is committed or invested and very little is reachable as cash, you are one surprise away from borrowing. Liquidity money you can actually get to quickly is what lets you meet a shock on your own terms instead of someone else's.

The fifth is **locked-up assets.** It is entirely possible to be wealthy on paper and stuck in practice, because the wealth can't be reached. Money tied up in hard-to-access retirement accounts, a single property, a concentrated holding of one company's stock, or a business you can't easily sell is real but it won't help you next month.

The sixth is the quietest: **a stuck mindset.** This is the rigidity that lives in your head an identity so fused with a certain lifestyle that downshifting feels like failure, a tendency to treat your current spending as a floor you can never go below rather than a choice you could revisit. Psychological rigidity is often the hardest to see and the most powerful, because it can keep you locked in even when the numbers would let you move.

Why you can't see it when things are good

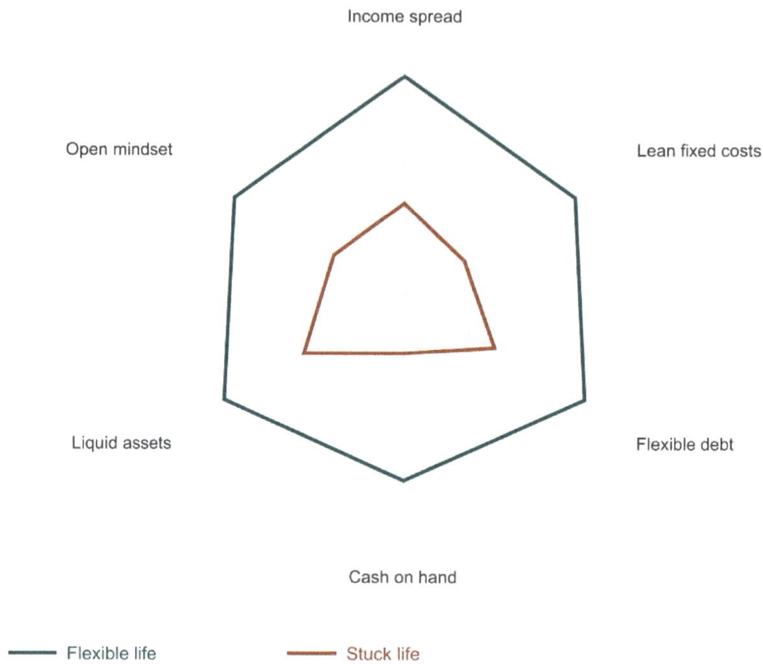

The shape of rigidity a flexible life reaches outward on every axis.

If rigidity is so dangerous, why don't more people notice it?

Because it is invisible in good weather. When income is steady and nothing is going wrong, every financial life looks fine the rigid one and the flexible one are indistinguishable from the outside, and often from the inside too. Rigidity only reveals itself under stress, which is precisely when it's too late to do much about it.

There's a mechanism underneath this that's worth naming, because it works on almost everyone: lifestyle inflation, and the way it ratchets. Each time your income rises, the new, higher spending quietly becomes your baseline the floor you now consider normal. The bigger place, the nicer car, the upgraded everything settle in and start to feel like necessities rather than the luxuries they were a year ago. Commitments expand to fill the income available, and the breathing room you used to have disappears without your ever deciding to give it up. The ratchet turns one way on its own. Turning it back the other way takes deliberate effort.

The Rigidity Audit

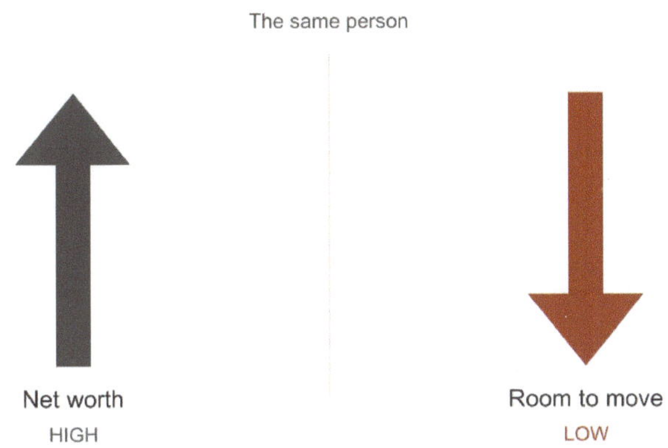

You can score high on what you own and low on room to move.

So if rigidity hides in good times, the answer is to go looking for it on purpose. That's what the **Rigidity Audit** is a structured, honest look across those same six areas, asking one question of each: is this *flexible, tightening,* or *locked?*

Income: is it spread across more than one source, or riding on a single point of failure? Fixed costs: what share of your income is committed before the month even begins? Debt: could you pause or reduce it if you had to? Cash: how many months could you cover from money you can actually reach? Assets: how much of your wealth could you get to within a week without a penalty? And mindset: which parts of your current life do you treat as permanent that are, in fact, choices?

The point of the audit isn't a score to feel bad about. It's a map. Almost no one is rigid everywhere most people are flexible in some areas and quietly locked in others, and the value of looking is that it shows you *where to create room first.* You don't have to fix everything. You have to find the one or two locked areas that would hurt the most and start there. Later in the book, this same six-part view becomes a sharper, more quantified tool; for now, the goal is simply to see the shape of your own rigidity clearly.

Broke is not the same as stuck

It's worth pausing on a distinction that quietly trips up a lot of smart people, because confusing these two leads to solving the wrong problem.

Broke means you don't have enough. The numbers are too small; more income or less debt is the answer. *Stuck* means you may have plenty, but you can't move it when you need to. These are different conditions with different cures, and net worth doesn't tell them apart. Net worth measures what you *have.* Flexibility measures what you can *do* with it when life changes. A person can have a large, healthy net worth and almost no room to move Marcus, from the last chapter, was exactly that. And a person with a modest income can be remarkably flexible: low fixed costs, real cash on hand, few locked commitments, and the willingness to adjust. The second person is, in every way that matters under pressure, in better financial health than the first.

This is why "just earn more" is such incomplete advice. More income, poured into the same rigid structure, often just builds a larger, more expensive trap. The goal isn't only a bigger number. It's a number you can actually move.

You got stuck by accident you can get unstuck on purpose

If there's a comforting truth in this chapter, it's this: nobody chooses rigidity deliberately. It accumulates one reasonable decision at a time, mostly during good years when it costs nothing to take on. Which means it isn't a verdict on your character, and it isn't permanent. Every locked area you found in the audit can be loosened, on purpose, with intention and the rest of this book is the how.

Consider Priya. Five years ago she earned a third less than she does now and felt stretched. Today she earns more and feels just as stretched maybe more. No single decision did it. A nicer apartment when she got promoted. A car payment that seemed reasonable at the time. Two streaming services, then four. A gym membership she uses twice a month. Each choice was small and sensible on its own, and each quietly became permanent. When a recruiter offered her a fascinating role that paid slightly less, she found she couldn't take it her fixed costs had grown to swallow her raise. She hadn't decided to trap herself. She'd simply never decided not to. That's how almost everyone gets stuck: not in one bad move, but in a hundred un-reversed small ones.

But flexibility is not one-size-fits-all. The kind of room you most need to build depends on the kind of conditions you're facing and learning to read those conditions is where we go next.

Chapter summary:

- Financial fragility usually comes from rigidity, not from low income; plenty of people look successful and are deeply stuck.
- Money gets stuck in six places: income concentration, high fixed costs, rigid debt, a thin cash cushion, locked-up assets, and a stuck mindset.
- Rigidity is invisible in good times and shows up only under stress; lifestyle inflation ratchets it tighter with every raise.
- "Broke" and "stuck" are different conditions with different cures you can have a high net worth and still have no room to move, and every locked area is reversible on purpose.

Questions to think about:

- Run the six-area Rigidity Audit on yourself. Which areas feel flexible, which are tightening, and which are locked?
- Which single locked area would hurt the most if a shock hit tomorrow?
- How much of your income depends on one employer, one client, one skill, or one market?
- If you had to cut your spending by a quarter within sixty days, what could move and what couldn't?

Chapter 3 · The Bend-Don't-Break Mindset

There are two very different things we call financial strength, and confusing them is one of the most expensive mistakes a person can make.

The first kind is the strength of something solid and unmoving a thick wall, a heavy beam, a fortress. It feels powerful precisely because it doesn't budge. The second kind is the strength of something that can take a hit and recover a reed in the wind, a suspension bridge, a boxer who rolls with a punch. It doesn't resist force so much as absorb it and spring back. We tend to admire the first kind and underestimate the second. But put both in front of a strong enough storm, and it's the rigid one that cracks while the flexible one bends and survives.

In money, these two strengths have names. The first is *stability* being fine as long as nothing changes. The second is *agility* being fine when everything does. They look identical in calm conditions. They could not be more different in a storm. And since we established in the last two chapters that change is now the rule rather than the exception, it's worth being clear about which strength actually protects you. It's the second one.

Strength that bends

Two kinds of strength meet the same force; the rigid one cracks.

We've been taught to read flexibility as weakness as softness, compromise, a lack of conviction or discipline. So it's worth correcting that at the root, because the whole book depends on it.

In engineering, flexibility isn't the absence of strength. It *is* strength, deliberately designed in. Tall buildings are built to sway, sometimes by several feet at the top, because a tower that refused to move would shatter in a high wind. Bridges are given expansion joints so they can stretch and contract with heat instead of buckling. An aircraft wing flexes in turbulence on purpose; a wing that couldn't would snap. In every one of these cases, the engineers didn't add flex because they ran out of strength. They added it *because* it makes the structure stronger able to meet force by moving with it rather than standing rigidly against it until it breaks.

A financial life works the same way. Keeping slack in your budget, holding cash you're not "putting to work," staying able to change course none of that is being undisciplined or unambitious. It's the design choice that keeps the whole structure standing when the wind comes. "Bend, don't break" is not a fallback. It's the plan.

The four kinds of money weather

The four kinds of money weather, each asking a different response.

You can't prepare for conditions you can't name. So before any tactics, it helps to name the conditions because every financial life, no matter how different, moves through the same four kinds of weather, and each one asks something different of you.

Normal weather is the calm. Income is steady, expenses are predictable, nothing urgent is happening. This is most of life, and it's the most misunderstood of the four, because it feels like nothing is required the unremarkable months when the paycheck lands, the bills clear, and it is tempting to think money needs no attention at all. In fact it's the only time you can comfortably build flexibility which means doing nothing in normal weather is itself a decision, and usually the wrong one.

Storm weather is a shock. A job ends, a market falls, a large unexpected bill lands, an emergency hits. Force is striking your finances directly. In a storm the job is not to optimize or maximize it's to absorb the blow and protect what matters, calmly and quickly.

Opportunity weather is the one people forget to plan for. A rare chance appears: an investment worth making when others are fearful, a job offer, a business opening, a moment to buy something valuable at a discount because everyone else is forced to sell. Opportunity weather rewards only those who kept enough room cash, flexibility, attention to actually move when it arrives.

Transition weather is change you can see coming, at least partly. Marriage, a child, a move, a career pivot, caring for a parent, retirement. These aren't shocks; they're turns in the road, and they reward deliberate redesign *before* the change locks in, rather than scrambling to adjust afterward.

Reading the weather

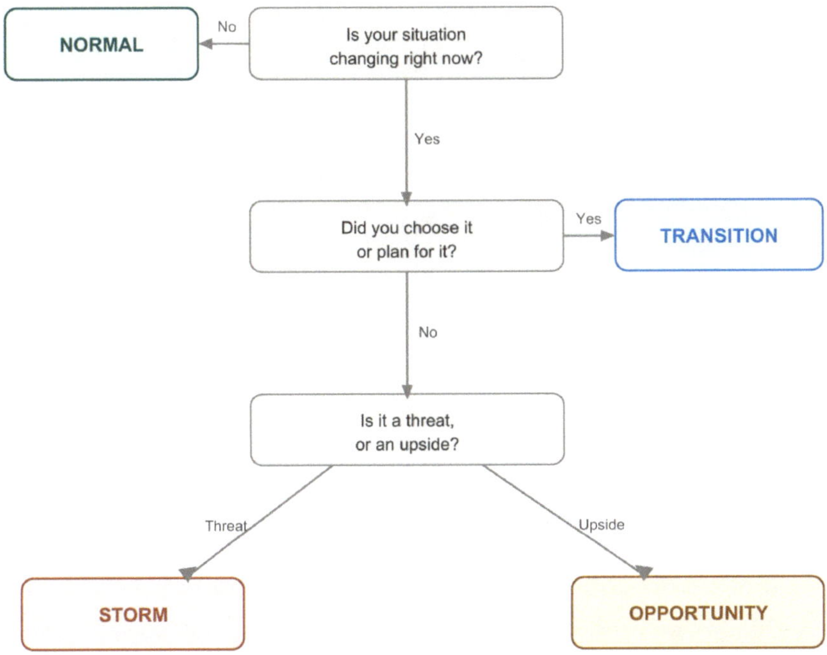

A quick read of which weather you're in right now.

Most of the costly mistakes in money come from misreading the weather using the wrong playbook for the conditions you're actually in.

Some people run storm tactics in normal weather: they hoard, they panic, they refuse every reasonable risk because a crash might come, and they spend years braced against a threat that isn't there. Others run normal-weather habits straight into a storm: the income drops or the warning signs flash, and they carry on exactly as before, as if nothing has changed, until the situation forces a much harder adjustment. And a great many people sail into a major transition a baby, a relocation, a retirement treating it like ordinary weather, and only redesign their finances long after the change has already reshaped their lives.

The fix isn't a perfect forecast. It's the simple habit of stopping to ask: *what weather am I actually in, and am I using the right playbook for it?* A rough, honest read beats a precise answer to the wrong question. Is your situation changing at all? If not, you're in normal weather prepare. If it is, did you choose it? A change you're steering into is a transition. A change happening to you is either a storm, if it's a threat, or an opportunity, if it's an opening. Four questions, four kinds of weather.

A different response for each and mostly calm

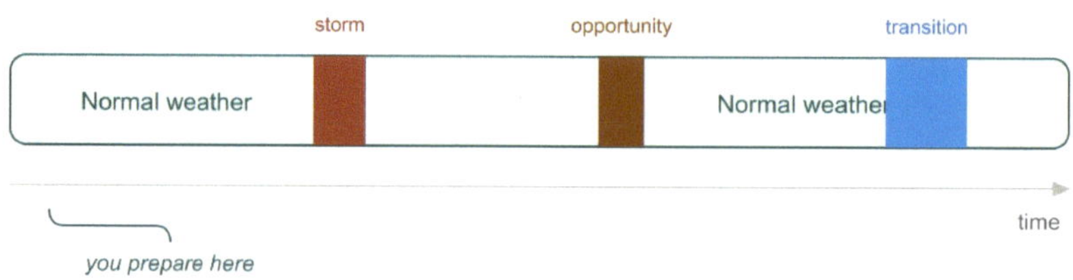

Most of a financial life is calm, punctuated by storms, chances, and turns.

The reason all of this matters is that you should not run your money the same way in all four kinds of weather. The real skill is switching modes as the conditions switch and that, not coincidentally, is exactly how the rest of this book is built. There's a part for adapting in normal weather (building the flexibility), a part for protecting through storms, a part for growing when opportunity appears, and a part for the major transitions. You're not learning one playbook. You're learning four, plus the judgment to know which is in season.

Consider two neighbors, Lena and Tomas, laid off the same month. Tomas treated it as a catastrophe to be survived by sheer will: he kept spending as before, certain something would turn up, and burned through his savings in a slow panic. Lena read it for what it was a storm and shifted her whole posture: she cut discretionary spending to the bone within a week, leaned on the buffer she'd built, and used the freed-up time to retrain rather than grab the first job offered. Six months on, Tomas was deeper in debt and back in a role he disliked; Lena had moved into better-paid work she'd actually chosen. Same shock, same starting savings. The whole difference was in how each one read the weather and matched the response to it.

And here is the genuinely reassuring part. Most of life is normal weather. Storms, opportunities, and transitions punctuate it, but they are the punctuation, not the sentence long calm stretches interrupted by occasional drama. That's good news, because the calm is precisely when the preparation has to happen. You cannot build an emergency fund during the emergency. You cannot create the flexibility to seize an opportunity in the same week it appears. The work of becoming agile is almost always done in the quiet, for the sake of the moments that aren't.

The mindset, finally

Bend-don't-break is, in the end, a posture toward the world. You stop being surprised that conditions change. You read the weather honestly instead of assuming permanent sunshine or bracing for permanent storms. You do the unglamorous work of preparing in the calm. And you keep enough room to move that a storm can't break you and an opportunity can't slip past you.

It isn't pessimism, which spends the good days waiting for the bad ones. And it isn't naive optimism, which assumes the good days will simply last. It's something steadier than either: realism with give built into it.

Reading the weather, though, only tells you what's happening around you. It doesn't tell you what *you* should do about it especially in the moments when fear, urgency, or comparison are loudest. For that, you need a compass of your own. That's where we go next.

Chapter summary:

- Stability (being fine when nothing changes) and agility (being fine when everything does) look the same in calm conditions and behave completely differently under stress; agility is the strength that protects you in a changing world.
- Flexibility is engineered strength, not weakness towers sway, bridges flex, and wings bend on purpose, because moving with force beats standing rigidly against it.
- Every financial life moves through four kinds of money weather: normal, storm, opportunity, and transition and each asks for a different response.
- Most life is normal weather, which is exactly when flexibility must be built; you can't dig the well during the drought.

Questions to think about:

- Which kind of money weather are you in right now? Which were you in a year ago?
- Are you running the right playbook or bracing for a storm in calm weather, or coasting through a storm as if it were calm?
- If a storm hit this month, how many months could you weather it before something broke?
- If an opportunity appeared next week, would you have the room cash, flexibility, attention to take it?

Chapter 4 · Your Money Manifesto

Picture the moment a real money decision lands on you.

The market is falling and your investments are down twenty percent, and every instinct says *do something.* Or a friend just tripled their money on something you don't fully understand, and the fear of missing out is loud. Or a large, tempting purchase is right in front of you and you could technically afford it. Or a windfall arrives and a dozen voices have opinions about what you should do with it. In that moment pressured, emotional, often rushed something decides for you. The only question is what.

For most people, what decides is whatever is loudest: fear, comparison, urgency, the most recent headline, the opinion of the person in the room who sounds most confident. The people who navigate these moments well are rarely smarter or naturally calmer. They've simply decided, in advance and in calm, what they actually value so the decision is half-made before the pressure ever arrives. That advance decision is what I'm calling a money manifesto, and writing yours is the last piece of groundwork before we start building.

Why values come before tactics

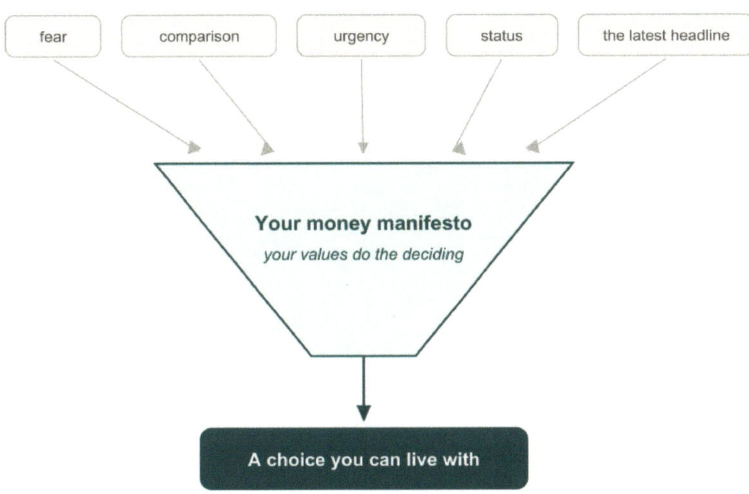

Under pressure something always decides; a manifesto lets your values do it.

The rest of this book is full of tactics, and they work. But a tactic is an answer to the question *what should I do?* and that answer changes with circumstances. Underneath every tactic sits a prior, more important question: *what do I want my money to do for me in the first place?* If you haven't answered that one, you'll apply the tactics inconsistently, bend them to whatever you already wanted, and abandon them the moment they get uncomfortable.

Here's the thing about a high-pressure decision: something always fills the vacuum. If your values aren't there to do it, fear will, or comparison will, or sheer urgency will. A manifesto is how you make sure the thing filling that vacuum is something you actually chose.

And it matters because most money decisions are not math problems. They are conflicts between two things you genuinely care about: security versus opportunity, spending now versus saving for later, freedom versus status, your future versus your present. The numbers can't resolve those for you, because both sides have real value. What resolves them is knowing which way you lean when they collide. That's what values are not lofty ideals, but tie-breakers for the moments when two good things pull in opposite directions.

What a money manifesto is

A Money Manifesto

Responding to change
over following the plan

A working money life
over the perfect budget

Continuous small moves
over big, rare overhauls

Values and people
over status and stuff

While both sides have worth, when they pull against each other, we choose the left.

A starter manifesto borrow it, argue with it, make it yours.

When software teams found themselves swamped by constant change, they didn't respond by writing a thicker rulebook. They wrote something much shorter: a manifesto, a handful of lines stating what they valued most when priorities competed. Crucially, each line took the form "we value A over B" not "B is forbidden," but "when A and B pull against each other, we choose A."

A money manifesto is the same idea pointed at your finances. A few short lines, entirely personal, naming what you value most when values compete. It is a compass, not a map. A map tries to chart every turn in advance, which is exactly what the changing world keeps invalidating. A compass just tells you reliably which way is north and that's all you need to keep orienting yourself, no matter how the terrain shifts.

It has to be short. If your manifesto runs to a page, it will never surface in the three seconds you have before you click "buy" or "sell." Four lines you can actually remember will do more for you than four pages you can't.

Four values to start from

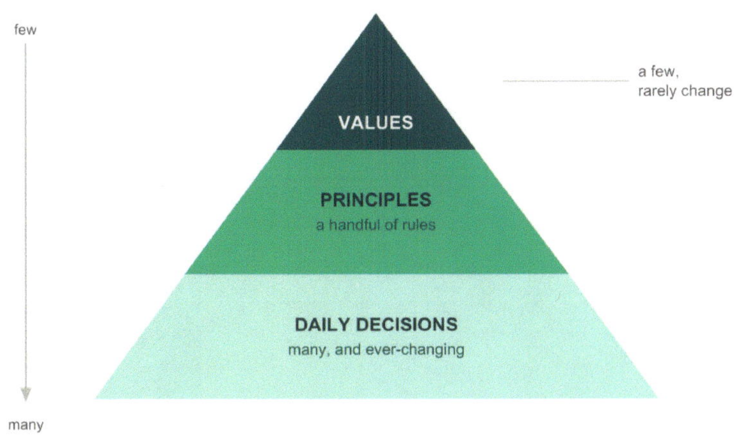

A few values shape principles, which settle the many daily decisions.

Here are four to react to not to adopt wholesale, but to argue with until they become yours. Notice what each one actually does to a decision.

Responding to change over following the plan. In practice: when the facts change, you change with them, and you refuse to treat that as failure. The person without this value clings to a plan out of pride long after it stopped fitting.

A working money life over the perfect budget. In practice: you'd rather have a good-enough system you actually use than a flawless one you abandon in three weeks. Done and imperfect beats ideal and theoretical.

Continuous small moves over big, rare overhauls. In practice: you make small adjustments often, rather than ignoring money for a year and then attempting one dramatic, exhausting fix that doesn't stick.

Values and people over status and stuff. In practice: when a purchase is really about looking successful to others, you're able to name that honestly and then decide on purpose instead of on autopilot.

The point of the "over" is honesty about trade-offs. There is nothing wrong with a plan, a budget, or nice things; all of them have real worth. The manifesto simply says which side you lean toward when they genuinely conflict, so you're not relitigating your entire philosophy every time a decision gets hard.

From values to principles

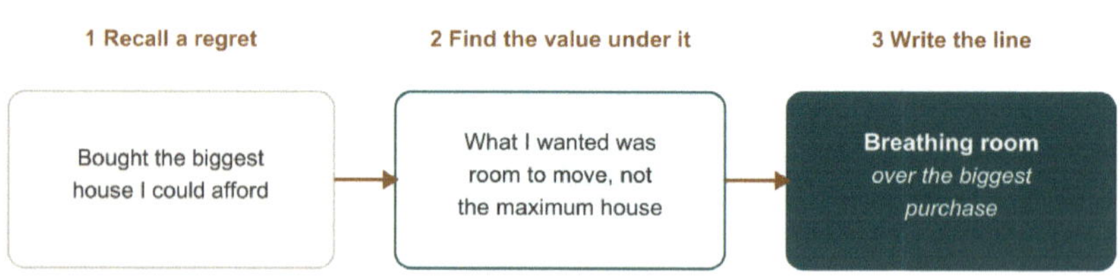

Mine a regret for the value underneath, then phrase it as a rule.

Values point a direction; they don't quite tell you what to do on a Tuesday. That's the job of principles the rules that turn a value into a behavior.

A value like "a working money life over the perfect budget" becomes a principle like *automate the essentials so they don't depend on willpower.* "Continuous small moves" becomes *spend fifteen minutes on money once a week.* "Responding to change" becomes *keep enough cash to absorb one major surprise.* "Values over status" becomes *wait a week before any large discretionary purchase.* Each principle is small, concrete, and checkable in a way a value isn't.

This is a hierarchy, and the shape of it matters. At the top sit a few values that almost never change. Below them, a handful of principles that change occasionally. At the base, the countless small decisions of daily life, which change constantly. The higher up you get something right, the more it quietly settles everything below it fix your values and the principles get clearer; fix your principles and the daily decisions get easier and far less tiring.

How to write your own

Don't start from a blank page, and don't just copy mine. The most useful manifesto is mined from your own history, because that's where your real values already left fingerprints.

The process is short. First, recall a few money decisions you're genuinely proud of, and a few you regret. Second, for each one, ask what value was honored or betrayed and pay special attention to the regrets, because a regret is almost always a value you abandoned under pressure. Third, phrase that value as an "A over B" line, naming the very thing it has to beat. Fourth, stop at about four lines. A manifesto you can recite in a hard moment is worth more than a comprehensive one you can't.

Done honestly, this should feel a little uncomfortable and unmistakably yours. If it reads like something you'd put on a poster for other people to admire, you've written aspirations, not values. Values are the things you'd actually choose when it costs you something.

Using it

Once it exists, your manifesto becomes the filter for everything that follows in this book. Every buffer you build, every expense you cut, every debt you weigh, every investment you make, every transition you steer through all of it runs through the same question: *which option honors my manifesto?* When a decision is hard, you're no longer starting from zero and hoping reason wins out over panic. You're checking a compass you set in advance.

Consider Aisha. She'd written a one-line money manifesto she half-thought was a gimmick: *we protect our freedom before we upgrade our comfort.* Then a larger-than-expected bonus arrived, and with it the familiar pull to finally upgrade the car. Sitting with the decision, she reread her line. The car was comfort. The freedom move was topping up the buffer that might let her partner leave a draining job. Without the manifesto she'd have weighed two vague wants in the heat of the moment and probably bought the car. With it, the decision took thirty seconds and felt clean rather than effortful. The values had already decided; she just executed. That's what a manifesto is for not to inspire you, but to decide for you when you're least able to think clearly.

Re-read it when the weather changes, especially during transitions, which have a way of scrambling people's values right when clear thinking matters most. And revise it rarely, on purpose, and only in calm never in the heat of a decision, because revising your values mid-pressure isn't growth, it's just rationalizing the thing you already wanted to do.

That completes the groundwork. We've seen why a financial life has to bend, where yours may have quietly stiffened, how to read the conditions you're in, and now what you stand for when those conditions test you. The compass is set. From here, we build starting with the first and most freeing kind of flexibility there is.

Chapter summary:

- In any high-pressure money decision something fills the vacuum; a manifesto ensures it's your chosen values rather than fear, comparison, or urgency.

- A money manifesto is a few short "we value A over B" lines tie-breakers for when two things you care about collide. It's a compass, not a map, and it has to be short enough to remember under pressure.
- Values point a direction; principles turn them into concrete, checkable rules, cascading down into the many small decisions of daily life.
- Write yours by mining your own proud moments and regrets for the value underneath, phrasing each as an "A over B" line, and stopping at about four then use it as the filter for every decision that follows.

Questions to think about:

- Name two money decisions you're proud of and two you regret. What value sits underneath each one?
- Draft your four-line manifesto in the A-over-B form. Which line will be hardest to actually live by?
- When you've made a money decision under pressure, what usually drove it fear, comparison, urgency, or your values?
- Which single principle, if you truly followed it, would change your finances the most?

Part Two · Adapt: Build Flexibility Before You Need It

There is one thing to understand about adaptation before anything else, because it governs everything in this part of the book: you cannot create flexibility in the moment you need it.

The capacity to bend is built in advance, in calm weather, when nothing is going wrong and there is no obvious reason to bother. By the time the wind actually arrives the lost job, the sudden bill, the rare opportunity, the life that turns a corner the flexibility is either already there or it isn't. You can't install the give after the force has hit. This is why the work of adapting belongs to normal weather, and why so few people do it: in the calm, it feels unnecessary, and in the storm, it's too late.

The plainest phrase for that built-in give is *breathing room* the space between what you have and what you need, between what you earn and what you're committed to spend, between the life you live and the edge of what you can afford. Breathing room is deeply unglamorous. It produces nothing, earns no admiration, and in good times can feel almost like waste money not "working," a life not running at full capacity. It is also the single most freeing thing in a financial life, because breathing room is the room in which every future choice gets made. A life with no breathing room has no moves. A life with it can absorb a shock, take a chance, change direction, or simply say no.

This part is about deliberately building that room. And there are four places to build it the four chapters ahead.

The first is room in your **cash flow** the gap between what comes in and what goes out, which is the most basic breathing room of all. We'll build it by keeping things simple, because simplicity, as you'll see, is itself a form of flexibility. The second is room in your **spending** designing a lifestyle that can expand and contract on purpose, so that scaling back becomes a dial you can turn rather than a crisis you endure. The third is room in your **income** loosening your dependence on a single source, so that a shock to one stream isn't a shock to your whole life. And the fourth is room in your **obligations** handling debt so that it doesn't quietly mortgage away the future flexibility you're working to build.

None of this is dramatic. You will not feel like a financial genius for keeping a cash buffer or trimming a fixed cost you'd stopped noticing. There's no story to tell at dinner about the obligation you chose not to take on. But this is where agility actually comes from. Not from a brilliant move in the middle of a crisis by then your options are mostly set but from the unremarkable room you built, quietly, when nothing was wrong.

One reassurance about the spirit of all this, because it's easy to misread. Building flexibility is not the same as deprivation. This is not a part about cutting every pleasure, tracking every dollar, or shrinking your life to the smallest possible footprint. Adaptation isn't about having *less* it's about being less *locked in*. You can live a full, generous, enjoyable life and still keep real room to move. In fact, that combination is the entire point: a life you actually like, built so that you don't have to dismantle it the moment circumstances change.

So let's begin where flexibility begins with the simple, badly underrated power of breathing room.

Chapter 5 · Your Financial Breathing Room

Ask most people whether they have financial breathing room, and they'll answer a different question they'll tell you what they earn. But income and breathing room are not the same thing, and confusing the two is exactly why so many people who earn well still feel like they're suffocating.

Breathing room is the gap. It's the space between what comes in and what you've already committed to send back out the distance between your income and your obligations. Someone who earns a fortune and has committed nearly all of it to fixed costs has almost no breathing room. Someone who earns modestly but keeps their commitments well below their income has a great deal. The gap, not the income, is what you actually get to work with.

The gap is the goal

This gap is the most important number in your financial life that you probably don't track. It's what funds every other strategy in this book: the buffer that absorbs a storm, the cash that lets you seize an opportunity, the slack that lets your spending contract without pain. Every later move spends from this gap. So the first task of an adaptable financial life isn't to earn more or invest better it's simply to open a gap, and then protect it.

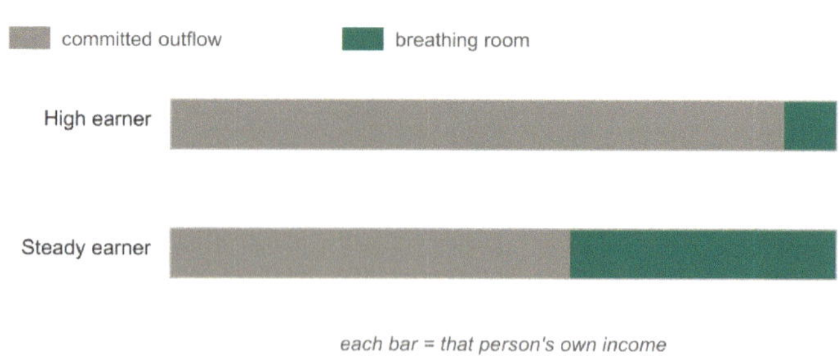

Breathing room is the gap, not the income. The higher earner here has committed almost everything and has little room; the steadier earner kept commitments low and has plenty.

Why breathing room feels like waste and why it isn't

Here's the catch: a gap looks, in good times, a lot like inefficiency. Money sitting in the gap isn't "working." Capacity isn't being used. Every instinct trained by a culture of optimization says to close it to put that money to work, to fill the space, to run your life at full throttle.

Resist that instinct, because slack is not waste. It's a shock absorber. Engineers don't load a bridge to its exact limit, and pilots don't plan a flight using every last drop of fuel they build in slack on purpose, because a system running at one hundred percent of capacity has no ability to absorb anything. The first bump breaks it. Your finances are no different. The gap that looks like wasted potential in calm weather is the only thing standing between you and a crisis in rough weather.

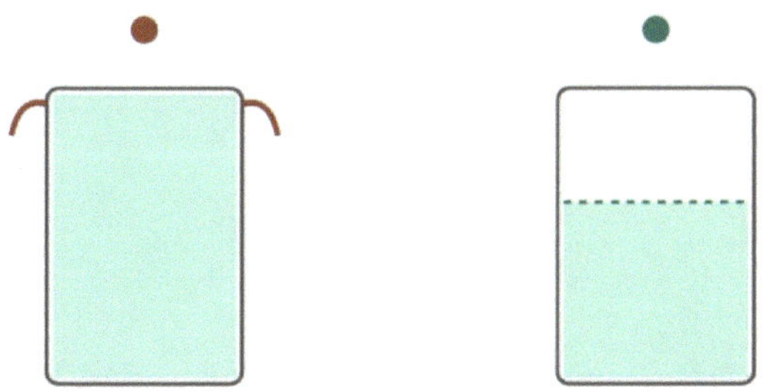

A cup filled to the brim overflows the moment anything extra arrives. A cup with headroom simply absorbs it. Breathing room is headroom.

Two levers, one focus

There are only two ways to widen the gap: bring more in or commit less out. Raising income matters, and we'll spend a whole chapter on it. But this chapter focuses on the other lever the committed, fixed portion of your outflow for a specific reason. Fixed commitments are what determine flexibility, and unlike a one-time spending cut, lowering a fixed cost widens your breathing room *permanently*, month after month, without any further effort. Trim one recurring obligation today and you've created room that keeps paying out for years.

Simplicity, the master tool

So how do you lower committed outflow and protect the gap without turning money management into a second job? The answer is the most underrated skill in personal finance: simplicity deliberately reducing the amount of money management you have to do at all.

Complexity is a quiet tax. Every extra account, subscription, card, and recurring commitment is one more thing to track, one more place money can leak, one more decision to make, one more part that can fail, and one more thing that quietly disrupts your focus. People assume a sophisticated financial life means a complicated one; many even take a quiet pride in justifying the complexity of their fixed costs. The opposite is usually true. A simple financial life fewer accounts, consolidated where it makes sense; fewer recurring commitments; the essentials automated has fewer leaks, fewer failure points, and far less drag on your attention. The goal is to maximize the money work you *don't* have to do.

How to Simplify

The method is unglamorous and effective. List every recurring outflow and every account you hold. Go through them one at a time and ask a single question: *does this earn its keep?* Cancel what doesn't. Consolidate what overlaps. Then automate what remains bills, savings transfers, the moving parts so the system runs without depending on you to remember it. Done well, this leaves you with a financial life you could manage in about fifteen minutes a week.

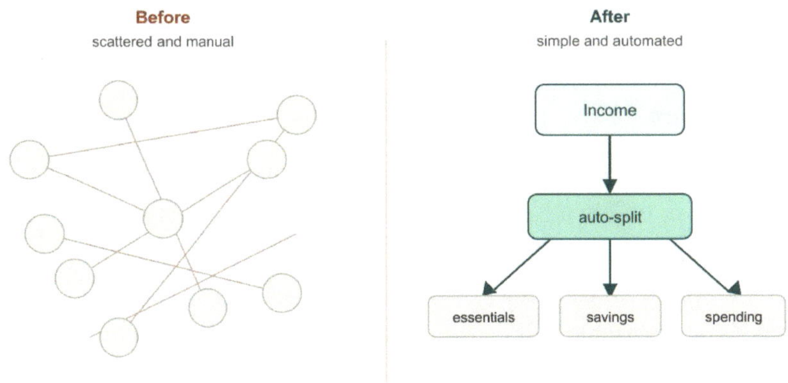

The same money life, two ways. Complexity scatters your attention and hides leaks; simplicity routes the essentials automatically and frees you to think about what matters.

Automation is pre-decided behavior

That last step automation is worth dwelling on, because it's where this chapter meets your manifesto. Automating a savings transfer or a bill converts a value into a behavior that happens whether or not you feel like it on a given day. "Pay yourself first" isn't a slogan; it's breathing room made automatic, the gap defended before you ever get the chance to spend into it. The less your breathing room depends on willpower in the moment, the more reliably it will be there when you need it.

Consider Marcus, a freelance designer whose income is lumpy some months double others. He built deliberate breathing room: the day any client paid, an automated transfer moved a fixed, modest amount into a separate account, and he lived on the rest. It felt almost too cautious in the fat months. Then a major client paid an invoice sixty days late. The old Marcus would have scrambled, taken a bad-fit rush job, maybe borrowed. The new Marcus barely noticed the room he'd quietly accumulated covered the gap, and he kept his pricing and his standards intact. He didn't need willpower in the hard month, because he'd pre-decided the behavior in the easy ones. The buffer wasn't idle money. It was the thing that let him say no.

This gap, kept simple and defended by automation, is the platform everything else in the book stands on. Without it, every later strategy is harder; with it, most of them get easier. But breathing room is a steady-state cushion it sits there, quietly absorbing. Real agility also needs spending that can actively *move*: contract quickly and calmly when the weather turns. That's next.

Chapter summary

- Breathing room is the gap between income and committed outflow the first and most basic form of flexibility, and it depends far more on your fixed commitments than on how much you earn.
- Breathing room can feel like waste, but slack is a shock absorber; a financial life run at full capacity has no room to absorb anything.
- You widen the gap by lowering committed costs (this chapter) or raising income (later); lowering a fixed cost widens the gap permanently.
- Simplicity is the master tool fewer accounts, fewer commitments, and automation reduce both the work and the fragility of your money, and automation turns your values into behavior that doesn't depend on willpower.

Questions to think about

- What is your real monthly gap between income and committed outflow and do you actually know the number?
- How many accounts, subscriptions, and recurring commitments are you carrying, and which would you not sign up for again today?
- Which of your fixed costs could be lowered once, permanently widening your breathing room?
- If you automated one thing this week, which would free up the most mental attention?

Chapter 6 · The Adaptable Spending System

A budget, for most people, is a plan for a life that doesn't change. It assumes a steady income and tries to arrange that income tidily across the month. As far as it goes, that's useful. But it answers only one question what *should I spend when things are normal?* and says nothing about the question that actually decides whether you bend or break: *what do I do when the income drops?*

An adaptable spending system answers the second question. It's built not to optimize a fixed life but to flex to expand a little in good times and, far more importantly, to contract quickly and calmly when the weather turns. The difference between the two isn't how much you spend. It's whether your spending can *move on command.*

The elasticity of an expense

Start with a property of spending that most people never think about: every expense has an elasticity a measure of how easily it can shrink or disappear. Some costs are sticky. Rent, a loan payment, and insurance don't bend much in the short term, no matter how badly you need them to. Others are elastic: dining out, subscriptions, and impulse purchases can drop to nearly zero almost overnight, with no contract and no penalty.

This matters enormously, because the elastic spending is your room to contract. When you need to cut, you cut from the elastic end first and the trouble is that most people have never sorted their spending this way. So when income drops and the pressure hits, they don't know where the give is. They freeze, or they cut at random, or they agonize over the wrong things while the easy wins sit untouched.

Every expense sits somewhere between sticky and elastic. The elastic end is your room to contract knowing where each cost falls is what lets you cut fast and in the right order.

Prioritizing your spending: the MoSCoW method

There's a simple way to do that prioritizing, borrowed from how teams prioritize when they can't do everything at once. It splits spending into four buckets: **Must Have, Should Have, Could Have,** and **Won't-have-for-now.**

Must Have is what keeps you housed, fed, and safe non-negotiable. **Should Have** is real quality of life: important, but survivable to pause for a while if you had to. **Could Have** is genuinely nice and entirely discretionary the first thing to go when a storm hits. And **Won't-have-for-now** is the things you've consciously decided not to spend on in this season, which keeps them off the table instead of nagging at you.

Prioritize your spending once, in calm weather, and the cut order is already decided: drop the Coulds, trim the Shoulds, and protect the Musts from the top down.

The power of doing this isn't the prioritizing itself; it's the timing. If you prioritize in calm weather, then in a storm the hard decisions are already made. You're not agonizing over what to cut while panicking about income you drop the Coulds, trim the Shoulds, and protect the Musts, in a sequence you set in advance, when you were calm enough to set it well.

Design the contraction before you need it

Take this one step further and build it into a number. Sketch a "lean mode" version of your spending today: what your month would look like if your income fell by a quarter, or a third. Which Coulds vanish, which Shoulds shrink, what the total comes to. Knowing that figure and having the list ready is the financial equivalent of locating the exits before there's any smoke. If a storm comes, you don't design your response under pressure; you just switch into a mode you already built.

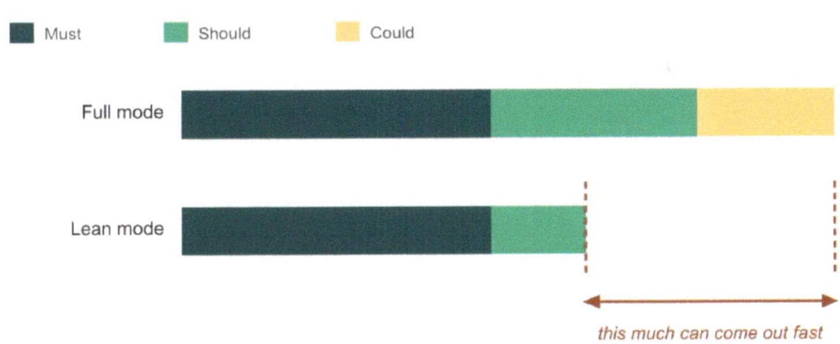

A lean-mode budget, mapped in advance: the Musts hold, the Shoulds shrink, the Coulds come out entirely. The gap between the two is how far you can contract fast.

Cutting without collapse

There's an emotional reason all of this preparation matters, not just a practical one. Cutting back, in the moment, feels like failure and loss like proof that something has gone wrong with your life and that feeling is exactly what makes people freeze when they most need to act.

Deciding in advance defuses it. When you decided months ago, in calm weather, that dining out was a "Could," then pausing it during a rough stretch isn't an admission of defeat it's simply executing a plan you made on purpose. The decision carries no shame, because you already made it when you were thinking clearly, and it costs no energy, because there's nothing left to decide. You've moved the hard thinking out of the worst possible moment and into the best one.

Expand on purpose, too

Adaptability runs in both directions, and the upside deserves equal attention. When good weather returns, an adaptable system lets you add things back but *deliberately,* choosing which Shoulds and Coulds are worth restoring rather than letting your spending quietly swell to fill the new room. This is your defense against the lifestyle ratchet from Chapter 2: the goal isn't to spend as little as possible forever, it's to enjoy more when you can without permanently locking it in. A good system lets you live well in the good times *and* shrink gracefully in the bad ones which is the whole point of building it to move.

There's a subtler move on the expansion side, too: when you do add spending back, bias it toward things that genuinely add value to *you* your health, your relationships, your skills, your peace of mind rather than toward status or autopilot upgrades. Increasing spending on what measurably improves your life isn't the lifestyle ratchet; it's the reward for building the room in the first place. The ratchet is mindless creep. This is its opposite: spending more, on purpose, on the few things that actually pay you back.

Consider Nadia, whose hours were cut without warning. Because she'd already sorted her spending into Must-, Should-, Could-, and Won't-have-for-now tiers months earlier, contracting took an afternoon, not a crisis: she paused every "Could," trimmed the "Shoulds," and protected the handful of "Musts" that kept her life functioning and sane. No agonizing, because the thinking was already done. What surprised her came later. When her income recovered, she didn't simply let spending drift back up she used the same map in reverse, deliberately restoring only the items that had genuinely added to her life and quietly leaving the rest paused for good. The contraction had taught her which of her old expenses she'd never actually missed. She came out the other side spending less and enjoying it more.

Spending that can contract protects you from below. But the deepest source of fragility for most people isn't on the spending side at all it's having every dollar of income riding on a single source. That's where we go next.

Chapter summary

- A normal budget optimizes a stable life; an adaptable spending system is built to expand and contract on purpose.
- Every expense has an elasticity, and prioritizing your spending in advance tells you what can move and in what order.
- The MoSCoW framework sorts spending into Must Have, Should Have, Could Have, and Won't-have-for-now, so that in a storm the cuts are already decided and made calmly rather than in a scramble.
- Build a "lean mode" version of your spending now, and in good times choose deliberately what to add back rather than letting lifestyle inflation fill the room.

Questions to think about

- Sort last month's spending into Must Have, Should Have, Could Have, and Won't Have. What surprised you about the size of each bucket?
- What would your "lean mode" budget look like if income dropped by a third and do you know that number today?
- Which "Coulds" have quietly migrated into feeling like "Musts"?
- In your last good stretch, did you add things back on purpose, or did spending just expand to fill the room?

Chapter 7 · Income That Can Move

If an investor put every dollar they owned into a single stock, we'd call it reckless no diversification, no protection, one company's fate deciding everything. Yet this is almost exactly how most people hold their income. A single employer provides one hundred percent of what they live on, and a single decision in a single office a layoff, a restructuring, a closure can switch off the entire supply at once. We diversify our investments as a matter of basic prudence, then leave the far larger asset, our income, completely concentrated.

Income concentration is the single biggest hidden fragility in most financial lives, and it's the thing that turns an ordinary storm into a catastrophe. Lose a job when your spending can flex and your costs are low, and it's a hard season. Lose that same job when it was your only source of income and everything was committed against it, and it's a crisis. The work of this chapter is to loosen that single point of failure to build income that can move.

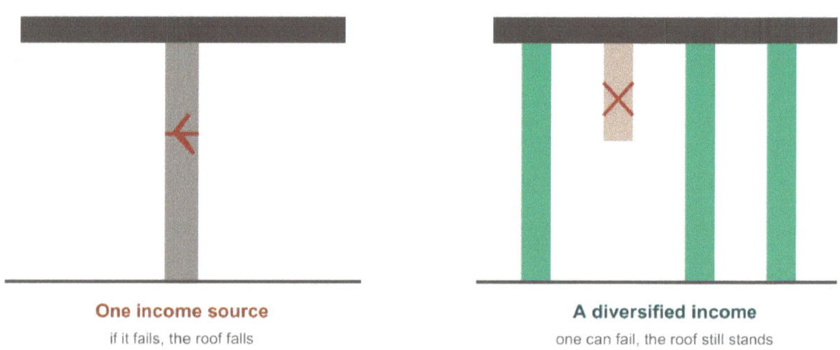

A roof on one pillar falls the moment that pillar fails. A roof on several stays standing even when one gives way. Your income is the pillar holding up your life.

Income as a portfolio

The reframe that changes everything is to treat your earning power the way you'd treat money you were investing: as an asset to be diversified. That does not necessarily mean working multiple jobs. It means spreading the risk across three dimensions the *buyers* of your work (more than one employer or client), the *skills* you can be paid for (more than one), and the *forms* your income takes (employment, freelance work, a modest side income, and so on).

Consider Ravi and Devi, a couple who looked equally secure on paper, both earning good salaries. But Ravi's income came entirely from one employer in one volatile industry, while Devi had spread hers: a core part-time role, a steady freelance client, and a small course she'd built that trickled in money each month. When Ravi's company restructured and his single stream went to zero overnight, the household wobbled hard. When Devi's freelance client later paused, she lost a slice, not the whole. Neither earned more than the other; Devi was simply harder to knock over, because no single failure could take everything at once. She thought about her income the way a careful investor thinks about a portfolio not chasing the highest possible return, but making sure no one event could end the game.

And the effect of even modest diversification is larger than people expect. A second stream that covers just part of your essential costs transforms a job loss from a cliff into a step down. You don't need a second income equal to your first; you need enough that the failure of any one source is survivable rather than total. Going from one source to two is a far bigger leap in resilience than going from two to three.

Career capital

Your skills are part of this portfolio too, and arguably the most important part. Skills that are current, transferable, and in demand are the difference between "if I lose this job I'm stuck" and "if I lose this job I have options." They are, in effect, income insurance and like all the work in this part of the book, the time to build them is in normal weather. The worst possible moment to start learning something new is the week you've been laid off and your attention is consumed by fear. Invest a little in your own capabilities while you don't need to, so that the capability is already there when you do.

Optionality your doors

Beyond skills sit relationships, reputation, and network and these are income insurance of a different kind. The people who recover fastest from a sudden income loss are almost never the ones who start networking after it happens.

They're the ones who quietly tended relationships for years before they needed anything, so that when they did, there were doors they could actually open.

That's a useful way to think about the whole thing: optionality is simply the number of doors you could open if you had to. Every current skill, every past client who'd take your call, every person in your field who knows your work is another door. Most of them you'll never use. But the security doesn't come from using them it comes from knowing they're there.

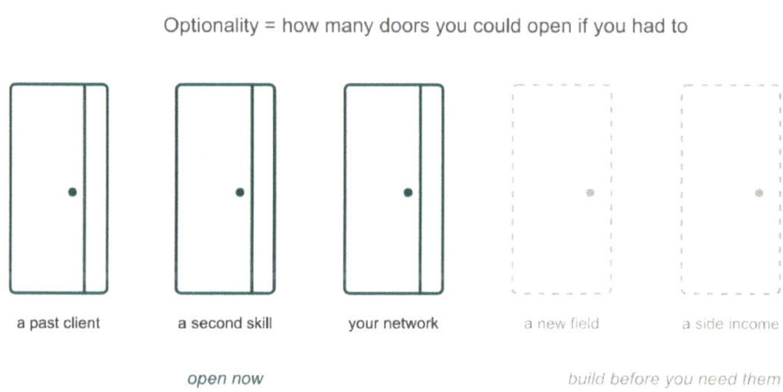

Every skill, client, and relationship is a door. You won't open most of them but resilience comes from how many you could open if a storm closed the main one.

Where to start

None of this requires becoming an entrepreneur overnight, and it shouldn't. The on-ramps are gradual, and you can start at whatever rung fits your life right now: keeping your existing skills sharp, tending the network you already have, adding a single adjacent skill, taking on one side client, and eventually building an income stream that doesn't depend on your main one at all. Each step up the ladder reduces your dependence on that single pillar. You don't have to climb it all at once; you just have to stop standing still at the bottom.

One practical principle ties this together: build optionality at a pace your weather can sustain. In calm, surplus stretches, push harder add a second income stream, invest in a new skill, widen your network while you have the slack to do it. In lean or stormy stretches, you don't abandon the project; you shift to maintenance, keeping the doors you've already opened rather than forcing new ones. Building options should never be so aggressive that it eats the very breathing room that makes you resilient. Match the ambition of your option-building to the weather you're actually in, and you'll keep widening your future without bankrupting your present.

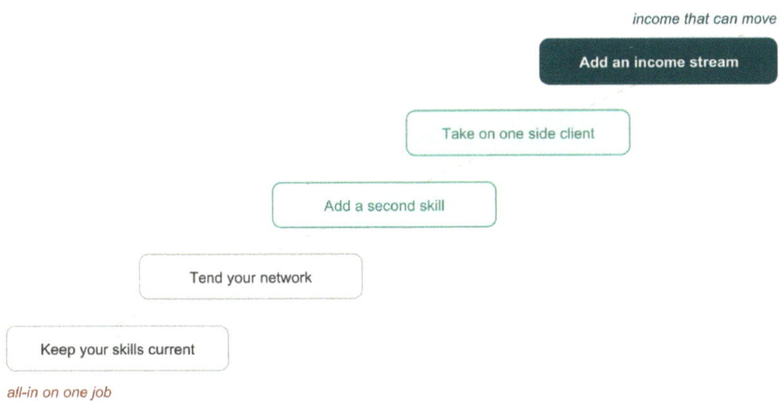

You don't have to leap from one income to many. Each rung reduces your dependence on a single source start wherever fits your life now.

Don't trade flexibility for new lock-in

One important caution, because it's easy to get this wrong. The goal of diversifying income is more flexibility, not more hustle for its own sake and a side venture that devours all your spare time, drains the very breathing room you built in Chapter 5, and saddles you with rigid new obligations can leave you *less* agile, not more. A second income that comes with its own crushing fixed costs is just a second pillar made of sand.

So diversify in ways that preserve your room to move. Favor income sources that are flexible, low-commitment, and built on skills you already have over ones that require you to mortgage your time and money to get started. The aim is resilience a life that can keep paying its way even when one source fails not simply more things to do.

With your income spread across more than one source, one major form of rigidity remains debt, which quietly commits your future income before it has even arrived. That's where we turn next, and it's the last piece of the foundation.

Chapter summary

- Most people would never hold all their savings in one stock, yet keep all their income in a single employer; income concentration is the biggest hidden fragility.
- Treat earning power as a portfolio diversified across employers or clients, skills, and forms of income so a shock to one part isn't a shock to all; going from one source to two is the biggest leap.
- Career capital (current, transferable, in-demand skills) and professional relationships are income insurance, best built in normal weather, before you need them.
- Diversify in ways that preserve flexibility; a side venture that consumes all your breathing room and adds rigid obligations can make you less agile, not more.

Questions to think about

- What share of your income comes from a single source and how fast could it disappear?
- If that source vanished tomorrow, how many other doors could you open, and how quickly?
- Which one skill or relationship, built over the next year, would most reduce your income concentration?
- Are your current "side" efforts adding flexibility, or quietly adding obligations that reduce it?

Chapter 8 · Debt That Doesn't Trap You

Most of us were taught to sort debt into two piles. Good debt buys things that grow or earn a home, an education, a business. Bad debt funds things that don't the vacation on a credit card, the car more expensive than you needed. It's a useful rule of thumb, and it isn't wrong. But for building an adaptable life it's incomplete, because it sorts debt by *what it buys* and ignores the thing that actually determines whether debt traps you: how much room it leaves you to move.

A "good" mortgage taken at the very top of your budget can lock you in place as surely as any bad debt a large fixed payment that doesn't shrink when your income does. Meanwhile a small "bad" credit-card balance you could clear any month barely dents your flexibility at all. So this chapter offers a different lens. Not good versus bad, but flexible versus rigid: *does this debt add room to move, or take it away?*

How debt removes room

Start with what debt actually does to your finances, mechanically. Every debt commits a piece of your future income before that income has arrived. The fixed payment lowers the breathing room you built in Chapter 5, and it shrinks how far your spending can contract in Chapter 6 because a loan payment, unlike dining out, doesn't move to the "Could" pile when a storm hits. The larger, more unavoidable, longer-lasting, and more rate-sensitive the payment, the more of your future it has already spoken for.

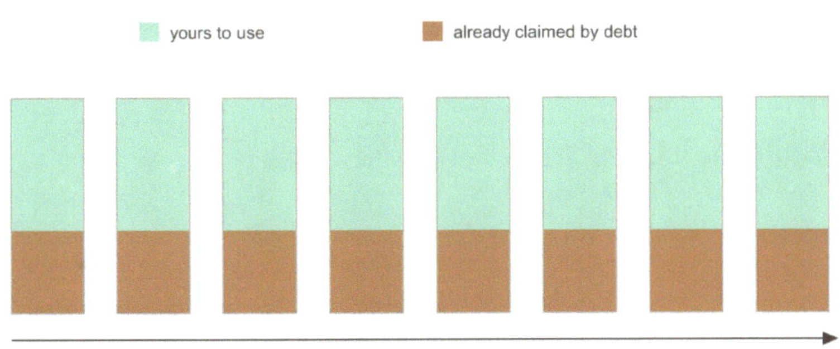

your next eight months of income — a slice of each is spoken for before it arrives

Debt spends your future income in advance. A slice of every month ahead is already claimed before you earn it and that slice can't flex when you need it to.

The Debt Flexibility Test

So instead of asking whether a debt is "good" or "bad," run it existing or proposed through five questions. How big is the fixed claim it makes on your monthly income? How *reversible* is it: can you exit, pause, refinance, or prepay without penalty? How much *rate risk* does it carry: is the payment fixed, or could it grow against you? *What does it buy* a productive asset and real options, or just pulled-forward consumption? And how long is its *duration* how many years does it commit you?

The Debt Flexibility Test. A debt that scores toward the right on all five small, reversible, rate-stable, productive, short barely dents your agility. One that scores left is a flexibility killer, whatever pile the old rule put it in.

A debt that's small, reversible, rate-stable, productive, and short adds almost nothing to your fragility. One that's large, rigid, variable, consumptive, and long is a flexibility killer regardless of which pile the old good-versus-bad rule would file it under. The label was never the point; the room is.

Fragile debt

The most dangerous category the test reveals has a name worth remembering: *fragile* debt, debt that's perfectly fine as long as everything goes right, and ruinous the moment something doesn't. A payment sized to your current income continuing forever. A variable rate that only works if rates stay low.

A balloon payment due on the assumption that you'll be able to refinance. Debt taken on to pay other debt. Fragile debt is the financial equivalent of building with no slack at all: it stands beautifully in calm weather and collapses in a storm which, of course, is exactly when you can least afford the collapse.

Debt that buys flexibility

None of this means debt is the enemy. Used deliberately, debt can actually *add* room to move. A low-rate, flexible line of credit kept open and unused is a backstop that buys you options in a storm. Financing a genuinely productive asset on terms you can exit can free up cash you'd otherwise have tied up. The test for "good" debt is identical to the test for bad: not what it buys or what it's called, but whether, on balance, it leaves you with more room to move or less.

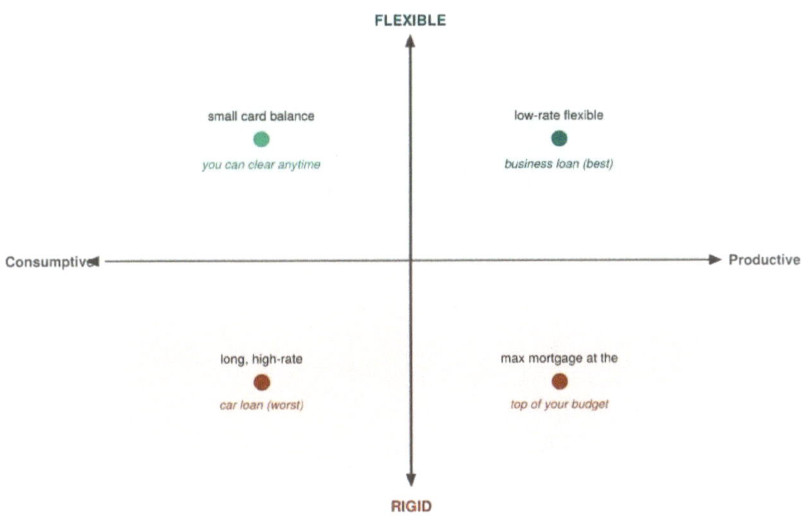

The old "good vs bad" split is only the left-right axis. Flexibility is the up-down axis and it often matters more: a "good," productive mortgage can still trap you if it's rigid.

A debt-flexibility plan

Putting it to work is straightforward. Run the test on each debt you carry, and rank them not by the usual math largest balance or highest rate but by how much room each one removes. Sometimes the most rigidity-creating debt isn't the biggest or the most expensive; it's the one whose fixed payment most limits your ability to adapt. Unwind the worst offenders first, refuse new fragile debt, and where you can, restructure what you keep toward more flexible terms a longer reversibility window, a fixed rate, a smaller claim. And remember that taking on debt is exactly the kind of high-pressure, future-shaping decision your manifesto from Chapter 4 exists to steady.

Consider two borrowers, Hana and Otto, who took on the same total debt. Otto optimized only for the lowest monthly payment, stretching everything as long as possible and treating the freed-up cash as money to spend. Hana cared about a different number: how fast she could become free if she had to. She kept one flexible, low-rate line she could overpay or pause, avoided locking herself into rigid long contracts, and quietly built room to accelerate. When both hit a rough year, Otto's "low payments" had become a cage he owed the same amount with no slack to move. Hana paused her overpayments, leaned on her built-in flexibility, and rode it out. Same debt on paper; one version trapped its owner and the other left her free to maneuver.

With breathing room built, spending made elastic, income diversified, and debt judged by the room it leaves you, you've now assembled all four kinds of flexibility the complete foundation of an adaptable financial life. That foundation is what makes it possible not just to bend, but to take a real hit and recover. Which is where the next part begins: Protect.

Chapter summary

- Debt isn't simply good or bad; what matters for agility is whether it adds room to move or removes it.
- Debt commits future income before it arrives, lowering breathing room and limiting how far spending can contract.
- The Debt Flexibility Test judges any debt by the size of its fixed claim, its reversibility, its rate risk, what it buys, and its duration not by category labels.
- The most dangerous debt is "fragile" debt that only works if everything goes right; used carefully, though, flexible debt can actually buy optionality.

Questions to think about

- Run the Debt Flexibility Test on each of your debts. Which one removes the most room to move?
- Which of your debts would become a problem if your income dropped or rates rose your "fragile" debt?
- Is any debt you carry buying real optionality, or just pulled-forward consumption?
- If you could restructure one debt toward more flexible terms, which would free up the most room?

Part Three · Protect: Build Strength for Setbacks

Up to now, this book has mostly been about the calm.

Part Two was the work you do when nothing is wrong opening up breathing room, making your spending elastic, spreading your income across more than one source, keeping debt from quietly trapping you. All of it was preparation, built in good weather for weather that hadn't arrived yet. This part is about the moment that preparation is finally tested: when the storm actually comes.

And it will come. This is the part of the book that asks you to accept something most financial advice tiptoes around: you cannot prevent every setback. A job will end. A market will fall. An illness, an accident, a family emergency, or a plain mistake will land on you at a moment you didn't choose. A few of these you'll see coming; most you won't. No amount of planning makes anyone immune, and any book that promises otherwise is selling something. The goal was never to avoid the hit. It's to be built to take it.

That's a different kind of strength than the flexibility we built in Part Two, and the difference is worth naming. Adapting is about having room to move *before* the force arrives. Protecting is about what happens at the moment of impact, and in the hard weeks that follow absorbing the blow without breaking, and then recovering your footing. The first is preparation; the second is resilience. You need both, and they are not the same skill.

There are four pieces to building it. The first is the set of buffers that take the initial blow the cash, the insurance, the backups that absorb a shock before it reaches the foundations of your life. The second is knowing what to actually *do* in the first ninety days of a real crisis, when fear is loudest and clarity is worth more than anything else. The third is how to recover from the setbacks you caused yourself the money mistakes without the shame and self-punishment that keep so many people stuck in the hole instead of climbing out. And the fourth is the inner game: the fear, the panic, the comparison that can turn a survivable setback into a genuine disaster, and how to keep your head when it counts most.

This is, in some ways, the most important part of the book, because it speaks to the fear that sits underneath all financial planning in the first place. Most people don't lie awake at night wanting to be rich. They lie awake afraid of being unable to cope of a blow they can't absorb, a hole they can't climb out of, a moment when the floor gives way and there's nothing underneath. The deepest reassurance money can offer was never a big number on a statement. It's the quiet confidence that whatever happens, you can take the hit and find your feet again.

That confidence isn't luck, and it isn't a personality trait some people are simply born with. It's built out of buffers, a plan, a healthier relationship with your own mistakes, and a steadier set of emotions under pressure. This part is how you build it.

So let's begin where every storm is met first with the buffers that take the opening blow.

Chapter 9 · Your Financial Shock Absorbers

When a financial blow lands, what happens next depends almost entirely on what stands between the blow and the foundations of your life. Two people can lose the same job, face the same bill, take the same hit and for one it's a stressful few months, while for the other it's a catastrophe that takes years to undo. The difference is rarely the size of the blow. It's whether they had anything in place to absorb it.

In a car, shock absorbers sit between the wheels and the cabin, soaking up the jolts of the road so they never reach the people inside. Your financial shock absorbers do the same job: they sit between a sudden blow and the essentials of your life, taking the impact so it doesn't crack the foundation. And like the ones in a car, they have to be installed before the road turns rough never during.

Defense in depth

The first thing to understand is that protection isn't a single thing; it's a stack of layers, each one catching what the layer before it couldn't. Engineers call this defense in depth, and it's why a serious system never relies on one safeguard. Your financial version has three layers wrapped around the foundation of your life.

The outermost and most-used layer is **accessible cash** the emergency fund that meets the common, ordinary blows. Behind it sits **insurance**, which catches the rare, catastrophic blows that no cash buffer could. And behind that sit your **backups and support** a credit line kept open, family or community you could lean on, other reserves the last line of defense for when the first two aren't enough. A blow hits the outer layer first; only what gets through reaches the next.

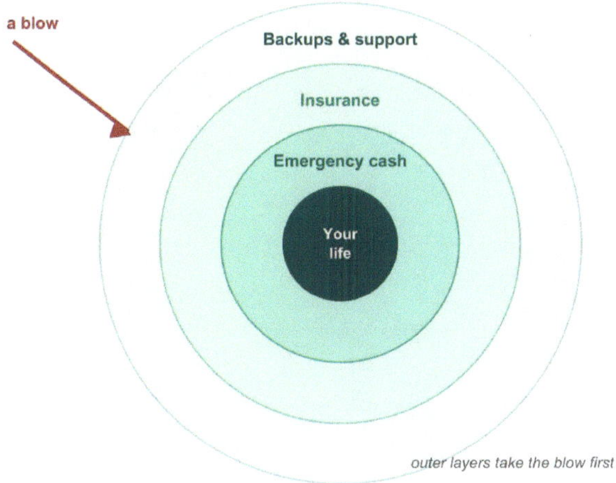

Protection works in layers. A blow meets your cash first, then insurance, then your backups and only what breaks through all three reaches the life at the center.

The first line: cash you can reach

The emergency fund is the layer you'll use most, and the one people most often get wrong by treating it like an investment. Its job is not to earn a return; its job is to *be there.* That means liquidity over yield money you can reach in a day, sitting somewhere boring and safe, not locked up chasing a few extra percent. The moment you need it, the only thing that matters is that it's available.

How much? Measure it in runway the number of months of essential expenses you could cover with no income at all. And here the work you did earlier pays off: your "lean mode" number from Chapter 6 is exactly the figure to divide into, because in a real storm you'd be running lean, not full.

Runway, measured in months of essential expenses. Under one month is exposed; three to six is building real resilience; beyond that you're well protected how far you aim depends on how steady your income is.

There's no universal right number, because it depends on how stable your income is. The income diversification from Chapter 7 matters here: the more concentrated or variable your income, the longer the runway you need, because your odds of a sudden gap are higher and your time to refill the tank is less certain.

The second line: transferring the risk

Some blows are simply too large for any reasonable cash buffer to absorb a serious disability, a major illness, a liability claim, the loss of a primary earner. You don't self-absorb these; you transfer them, which is all insurance really is: paying a small, predictable amount so that a rare, ruinous one becomes someone else's problem.

The rule of thumb is simple and clarifying: *insure the catastrophic, absorb the small.* Small, frequent costs a car repair, a dental bill, an appliance that dies belong to your cash buffer; insuring them just means paying a company to handle money you could handle yourself. Large, rare, potentially ruinous events belong to insurance. The mistake in both directions is common: people insure the small stuff they could easily absorb, and leave themselves dangerously exposed to the big stuff they never could.

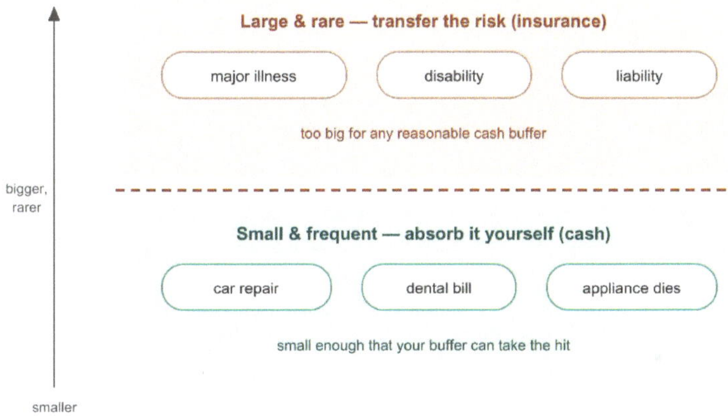

Match the absorber to the blow. Small, frequent shocks are for your cash buffer; large, rare ones are for insurance and the costly mistakes happen when people get this backwards.

The last line: backups and support

Behind cash and insurance sits a quieter layer that people rarely set up on purpose: the reserves behind the reserves. A flexible line of credit, opened and kept available before you need it, is one the productive, optionality-buying kind of debt from Chapter 8, sitting unused as a backstop. The willingness to lean on family or community is another. So is any resource you could turn to in a genuine emergency. None of these is your first move, but knowing they exist changes how a storm feels and the time to arrange them is in the calm, because the worst moment to go looking for a backstop is the moment you need it.

How much is enough?

Add it all up and the right amount of protection isn't a fixed figure it scales with your income stability, your fixed costs, the people who depend on you, and the insurance you already carry. The principle to aim for is this: enough that an ordinary storm becomes a manageable inconvenience rather than a crisis. And there is such a thing as too much. Fortifying endlessly hoarding cash you'll never need, insuring every conceivable risk has its own cost, in money not used and a life lived defensively. The goal is to be a shock absorber, not a bunker.

Consider Elena, who used to keep almost nothing in cash it felt like lazy money and invested every spare dollar instead. Then a medical issue collided with a slow stretch at work, and she had to sell investments at a loss, at the worst possible moment, just to cover ordinary bills. The lesson reshaped her thinking. She built her buffer up to roughly six months of bare-bones expenses, sized to her actual life: one income, some health risk, a job that wasn't bulletproof. It still felt like too much money sitting still. But the next time a shock came, she didn't sell a thing or borrow a cent the absorber soaked it up exactly as designed. "Enough" was never a universal number. It was however much let her sleep and stay invested through the bad months.

Shock absorbers take the blow. But when a serious storm does get through the job lost, the income gone you need to know what to actually do in the chaotic, frightening first weeks, when clarity is worth more than anything. That's the next chapter.

Chapter summary

- When a blow lands, the difference between a setback and a catastrophe is what stands between the blow and your foundations.
- Shock absorbers work in layers accessible cash for common blows, insurance for rare catastrophic ones, and backups and support as the last line.
- Cash's job is to be there, not to earn; size it in months of runway, and hold more if your income is concentrated or variable.
- Insure the catastrophic and absorb the small, build it all in calm weather, and aim for a shock absorber rather than a bunker.

Questions to think about

- How many months of essential expenses could you cover from cash you can reach this week?
- Which large, rare blows are you self-absorbing that you should be transferring with insurance or insuring that you could easily absorb?
- What is your last line the backups behind your backups and have you set it up before you need it?
- Given how stable your income is, is your runway too thin, about right, or so large it's holding you back from living?

Chapter 10 · The 90-Day Recovery Plan

The storm has arrived. The job is gone, or the business has stalled, or a bill has landed that changes everything. Your shock absorbers are doing their work the cash is buying you time but time is exactly the thing that now feels like it's running out. The question this chapter answers is the one that matters most in that moment: what do you actually *do?*

Here is the first and most important truth about a financial crisis: the danger is rarely just the event itself. It's the panic the event triggers, and the bad, fast, irreversible decisions panic produces. People drain retirement accounts in week one, take the first desperate offer, make a frightened call they can't take back not because those were the right moves, but because doing *something* felt better than sitting in fear. In a storm, clarity is worth more than cash. This chapter is about staying clear.

A loop for moving fast without panicking

You don't have time, in a real crisis, for the calm quarterly planning we'll build later in the book. You need something faster a way to move quickly without moving blindly. The military has one, designed for exactly this: high stakes, incomplete information, no time. It's called the OODA loop, and it has four steps you cycle through as fast as you can. **Observe** what is actually happening, stripped of the story your fear is telling. **Orient** work out what it really means for you. **Decide** on one clear next move. **Act** on it. Then immediately observe again, because the situation has changed, and run the loop once more.

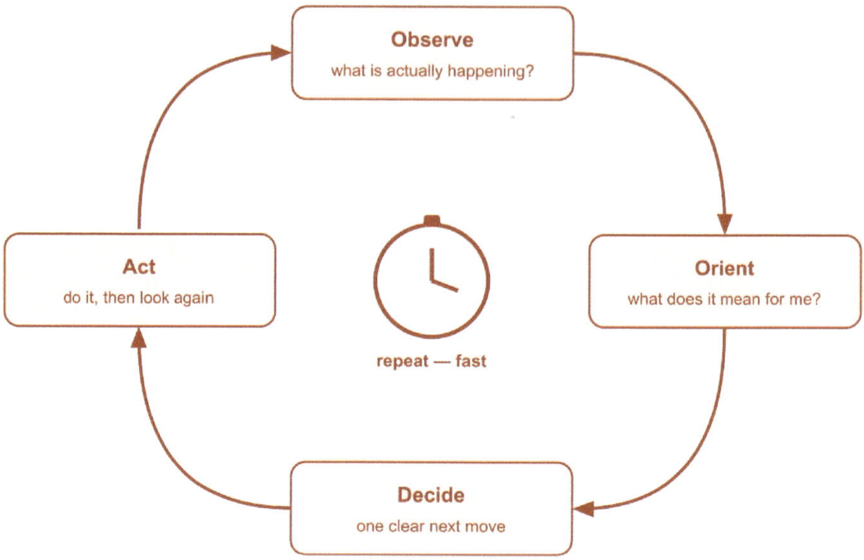

The OODA loop: a fast cadence for storms. Observe, orient, decide, act then look again. It channels urgency into a cycle instead of letting panic spend itself on one rushed, irreversible move.

What the loop gives you is a way to satisfy the urge to act which in a crisis is overwhelming without spending it all on a single panicked decision. Each turn is small and reversible. You're always moving, but you're moving in tight, correctable steps, re-checking reality every time, rather than betting everything on one big move made in the dark.

The first seven days: stabilize

Over a longer horizon, that loop organizes itself into three phases, and the first one is the one people skip at their peril. Before you fix anything, you stabilize you stop the situation from getting worse. In the first week, the goal is not to solve the crisis; it's to stop the bleeding and buy yourself room to think.

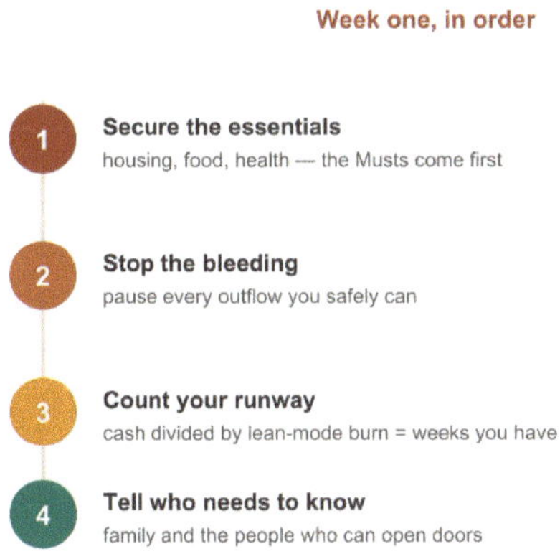

Week one has an order. Secure the essentials, stop the outflows you safely can, count your runway, and tell the people who need to know before you attempt anything clever.

Notice what isn't on that list: big, irreversible decisions. Week one is explicitly *not* the time to cash out investments, accept the first offer, or upend your life. Those are week-three decisions, made with a clear head and full information. Week one buys you the runway to reach week three without panic.

The full ninety days

From there, the recovery unfolds across about ninety days long enough to act deliberately, short enough to keep urgency alive. The shape is always the same: stabilize first, then assess, then rebuild.

clarity first, then options, then action — in that order

The 90-day recovery plan. Stabilize in week one, assess your options over the first month, then spend the rest rebuilding clarity first, then options, then action.

The middle phase assessing is where the work you did in earlier chapters pays off. This is when you open the doors from Chapter 7, run your spending through the Chapter 6 priorities, and lean on the buffers from Chapter 9. You map every option you have, prioritize ruthlessly, and choose a direction not the perfect one, just a clear one you can correct as you go. The final phase is execution: act on the plan, track it weekly, adjust as you learn, and, as soon as you can, begin rebuilding the very shock absorbers this storm just spent.

Why preparation beats willpower

The reason to have all of this worked out ideally before you ever need it is that a crisis is the worst possible time to design a response from scratch. Fear narrows your thinking exactly when you need it widest. A plan you decided on in calm weather does for a crisis what your sorted spending did for a budget cut: it moves the hard thinking out of the worst moment and into a better one. When the storm hits, you're not inventing a strategy through a fog of adrenaline. You're running one you already trust.

Consider Jordan, who lost his job with no warning. His first instinct was a frantic, around-the-clock hunt fueled by adrenaline exactly the willpower-driven sprint that burns out in two weeks. Instead, he ran the plan. Days one to seven: stabilize cut spending to essentials, map the runway, make the urgent calls. Then he stopped reacting and worked a steady ninety-day rhythm: assess what he actually wanted next, rebuild in deliberate weekly steps, protect his sleep and his buffer. By week six he wasn't desperate, so he could decline a bad-fit offer and hold out for a better one that arrived in week eleven. The recovery didn't come from heroic effort. It came from having a shape to follow when his willpower and his clarity were both at their lowest.

Sometimes, though, the storm isn't something that happened *to* you. Sometimes the setback is one you caused a mistake, a bad call, a season of poor decisions and recovering from that carries a weight the OODA loop doesn't address: shame. That's where we go next.

Chapter summary

- In a financial crisis the real danger is often the panic and the rushed, irreversible decisions it produces; clarity is worth more than cash.
- The OODA loop observe, orient, decide, act, then look again is a fast cadence that channels urgency into small, correctable moves instead of one big panicked bet.
- Week one is for stabilizing, not solving: secure essentials, stop the bleeding, count your runway, and tell who needs to know big decisions wait.
- Over ninety days the shape is always stabilize, then assess, then rebuild; a plan decided in calm weather beats willpower invented in a storm.

Questions to think about

- If your main income stopped today, what would your honest first move be and is it a stabilizing move or a panicked one?
- What is the one big, irreversible decision you'd be tempted to make in week one that's better left to week three?
- Right now, how many weeks of runway would your cash actually buy at lean-mode spending?
- Who are the people you'd need to tell and whose doors you'd want to open in the first days of a storm?

Chapter 11 · Recovering from Money Mistakes

Not every storm arrives from the outside. Some you cause yourself a bad investment, a purchase you couldn't afford, a debt you shouldn't have taken, a year you simply didn't pay attention. These setbacks carry a weight the others don't, and it isn't financial. It's shame. And shame, left unexamined, does more lasting damage to a financial life than almost any single mistake.

So this chapter is about the setbacks you can't blame on the weather and about the one skill that determines whether a mistake becomes a lesson or a life sentence: the ability to recover from your own bad decisions without punishing yourself into paralysis.

The trap isn't the mistake it's the shame

Here's what actually keeps people stuck. The mistake itself is usually survivable; people recover from lost money all the time. What they don't recover from as easily is the *story* they tell themselves about it that they're bad with money, that they always do this, that they can't be trusted with their own decisions. That story is shame, and shame has a predictable, destructive logic. It hurts to look at the mistake, so you avoid looking. Avoiding it means you don't understand it. Not understanding it means you're likely to repeat it. And repeating it deepens the very story that made you look away in the first place.

This is the shame spiral, and it's the reason the same mistake can lead to two completely different futures. The mistake is just a fork in the road. One path faces it; the other flees it and where you end up depends far less on the size of the error than on which path you take from it.

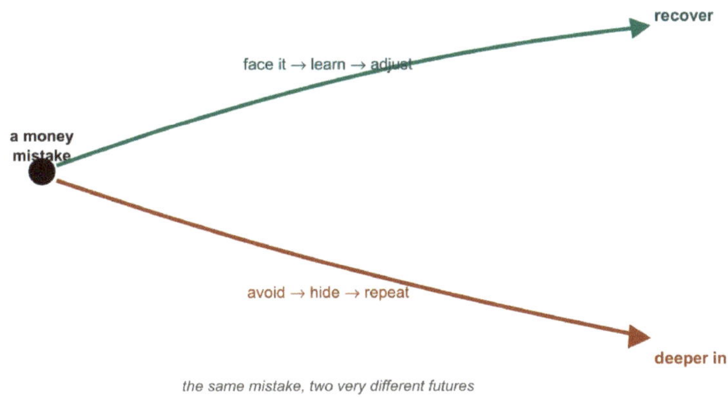

The same mistake, two futures. Facing it turns it into a lesson and a recovery; fleeing it into shame turns it into a spiral that repeats and deepens.

The blameless retro

There's a practice that breaks the spiral, and it comes, once again, from how good teams operate. When something goes wrong, strong teams run a *retrospective* a structured look back at what happened. But the best ones run it *blameless:* the explicit rule is that the review examines the decision and the system, never the worth of the person who made it. Not because nobody is responsible, but because the goal is learning, and people cannot learn from something they're busy defending themselves against. The moment a review becomes an accusation, the mind stops analyzing and starts hiding.

It helps to run this on a regular cadence rather than only after disasters: a brief monthly look back at your money decisions, plus a focused retro after any significant event a big purchase, a loss, a windfall. Made routine, it stops being a painful autopsy and becomes ordinary maintenance.

Run the same practice on your own money mistakes. It has just three questions. *What actually happened?* the plain facts, no judgment. *What can I learn from it?* the pattern or value underneath. *What will I change?* one concrete adjustment going forward. That's the whole tool. Notice what's missing: any question that begins with "why am I so…" Those questions feel like accountability, but they're just shame wearing a serious face, and they produce nothing but more of the spiral.

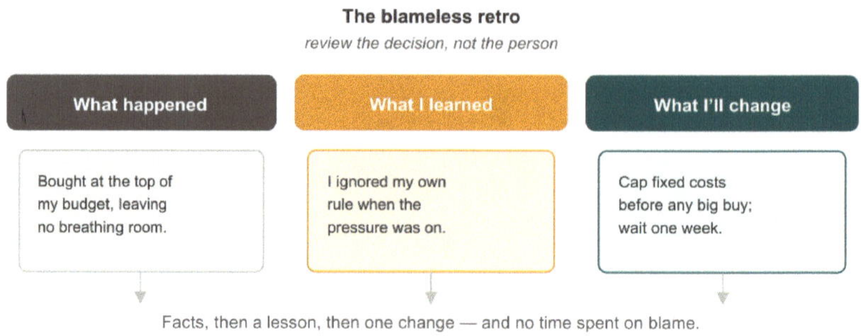

The blameless retro: three questions, no self-attack. Facts, then a lesson, then one change the same review a good team runs, pointed at your own decision.

You are not your mistake

Underneath the blameless retro is a distinction worth making explicit, because it is the thing shame refuses to allow: you are not your mistake. A bad financial decision is an *event* something you did, at a particular moment, with the information and emotions you had then. It is not an *identity*. "I made a bad investment" is a fact you can learn from. "I'm an idiot with money" is a story that makes learning impossible, because you can't fix a character; you can only fix a decision.

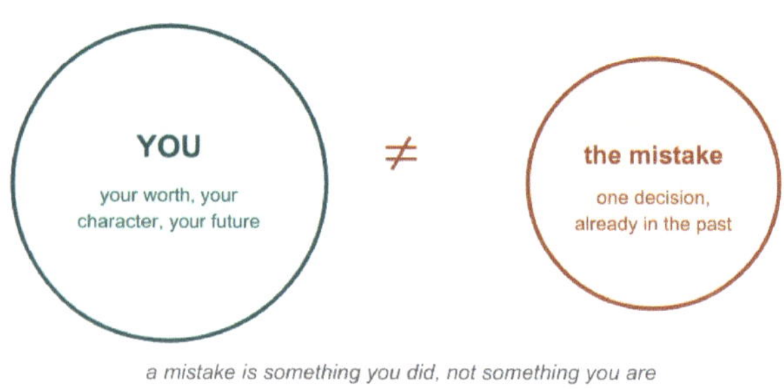

Keep the two apart. The mistake is one past decision; you are the whole person who made it and everything you do next. Collapsing them is what keeps people stuck.

Holding that line the decision over here, your worth over there is not letting yourself off the hook. It's the only stance from which real accountability is even possible, because it lets you examine the decision honestly without the examination feeling like an attack you have to flee.

The past is already spent

One more trap deserves naming, because it turns a single mistake into a series of them: the urge to justify a bad decision by doubling down on it. The money is already gone, or the years already lost, or the wrong path already walked some distance and the temptation is to keep going, to throw good money and time after bad, because stopping would mean admitting the first call was wrong. But the past is already spent. It cannot be recovered by any future decision, and it should have no vote in your next one. The only question that matters going forward is the same one from the recovery plan: given exactly where I am now, what is the best next move? Where you started has no bearing on it.

Rebuilding without self-punishment

Finally, resist the idea that you have to *suffer* your way back that a period of harsh self-denial is the price a mistake demands. It isn't. Self-punishment doesn't speed recovery; it slows it, because a person operating from shame makes worse decisions, gives up more easily, and hides more. The fastest way back is not penance but a clear-eyed retro, one concrete change, and the steady, unglamorous work of moving forward. Treat yourself the way you'd treat a friend who made the same mistake: with honesty, and without contempt.

Consider Caleb, who realized he'd quietly lost a meaningful sum to a string of impulse purchases and one investment he'd chased on a hot tip. His first reaction was the familiar spiral of self-disgust. Instead, he tried treating it like a blameless retro: not *what's wrong with me*, but *what in my setup let this happen, and what will I change?* Looking calmly, he saw the pattern purchases made late at night, the investment chased on a friend's say-so. So he changed the system, not just the resolve: a 48-hour rule on anything over a threshold, and a flat refusal to act on tips. The money was gone either way. But the Caleb who studied the mistake without flogging himself for it actually changed his behavior. The one who just felt ashamed would have repeated it.

All of this the shame, the spiral, the urge to flee or to punish points at something larger that runs underneath every financial decision you make: your emotions. They are always in the room, and in the hard moments they often hold the pen. Learning to work with them is the last piece of protection, and it's where we go next.

Chapter summary

- The lasting damage from a money mistake is usually not the mistake itself but the shame, which drives a spiral of avoiding, not learning, and repeating.
- A blameless retro breaks the spiral: ask what happened, what you can learn, and what you'll change and never "why am I so...," which is shame in disguise.
- You are not your mistake: a bad decision is an event you can fix, not an identity you're stuck with, and separating the two is what makes real accountability possible.
- The past is already spent and should have no vote in your next move; recover with one concrete change and steady work, not self-punishment.

Questions to think about

- Think of a money mistake you still carry. Have you run a blameless retro on it or are you still re-litigating your character?
- What is the story you tell yourself about your money mistakes, and is it a fact or an identity?
- Where might you be throwing good money or time after bad just to avoid admitting an earlier call was wrong?
- If a friend had made your worst money mistake, what would you tell them and why don't you say it to yourself?

Chapter 12 · Emotional Agility with Money

We like to think we decide with reason and merely feel our emotions on the side. With money, it's usually the other way around. Behind the spreadsheet, a feeling is almost always holding the pen fear when the market drops, envy when a friend pulls ahead, guilt about a past mistake, the quiet pressure to look as though you're doing well. These emotions aren't a flaw in your financial life; they're a permanent feature of it. The question is never whether you'll feel them. It's whether they get to make the decisions.

This is the last piece of protection, and in some ways the deepest, because all the buffers and plans in the world can't save a person who abandons them in a panic. Financial agility, in the end, rests on emotional agility: the ability to feel what you feel and still choose well.

The feelings that hold the pen

It helps to know the usual cast, because each one steers money in a predictable direction. *Fear* sells at the bottom and hoards out of dread. *Comparison* spends to keep up and takes wild risks to catch up. *Guilt* avoids the statements and soothes itself with purchases. *Status pressure* buys the signal rather than the thing. *Scarcity* clutches so tightly it can never invest in the future. None of these is irrational each one made sense at some point, often in a harder time. But left to run unmanaged, every one of them quietly nudges money toward a worse outcome than you'd choose with a clear head.

The pause

The instinct is to try to *suppress* these feelings to be coldly rational about money. That doesn't work, and it backfires; suppressed emotion just waits and drives the decision from underneath. Emotional agility is something different and more achievable. It's not the absence of feeling. It's the creation of a gap a small space between the feeling and the action.

Between the trigger and the response there is a space, and in that space sit all of your better tools: your values, your manifesto, your plan. The simplest way to open that space is to *name* the feeling. "This is fear talking" sounds almost too small to matter, but it does something real: it turns a feeling that is *driving* you into one you can *observe.* The instant you can see the emotion instead of just being inside it, the pause opens and the pause is where freedom lives.

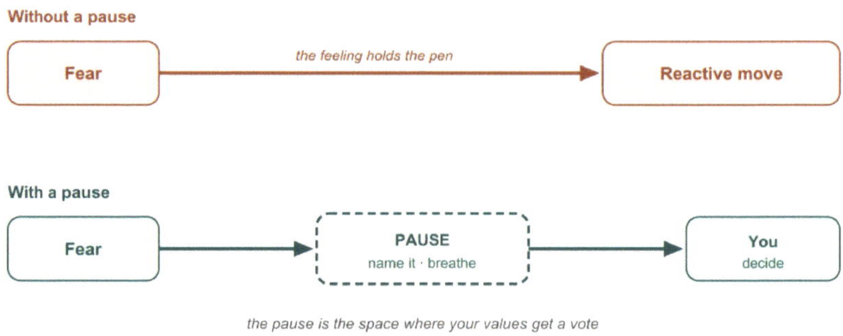

Naming a feeling opens a pause between the trigger and the response. Without it, the emotion acts for you; with it, your values get a vote.

Two kinds of fuel

Step back from individual moments and look at what motivates your money behavior over years, and you find two very different kinds of fuel. *Extrinsic* motivation comes from outside: comparison, status, the approval of others, the fear of falling behind. It's powerful, and it's also fragile, because it can never be satisfied someone always has more, and the goalposts move the moment you reach them. Chasing it is like running on a treadmill at full effort and never arriving anywhere.

Intrinsic motivation comes from inside: you handle money well because it matters to *you,* on your own terms. It's durable in exactly the way extrinsic motivation isn't, because it was never about beating anyone, so it doesn't collapse when the comparison changes. The same effort that goes nowhere on the treadmill becomes real progress when it's pointed at something that's actually yours.

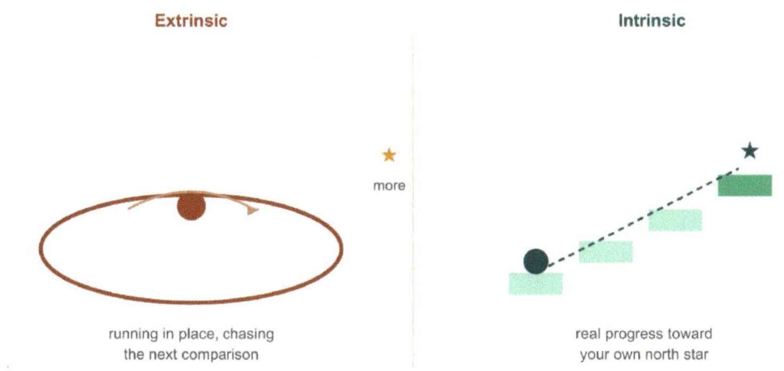

Extrinsic motivation is a treadmill maximum effort, no arrival, because the target keeps moving. Intrinsic motivation is a path: the same effort, but you actually get somewhere.

Autonomy, mastery, purpose

That durable, intrinsic fuel has three sources, and money can serve all three. **Autonomy** money that buys you choices and genuine control over your own life. **Mastery** the quiet satisfaction of getting steadily better at the practice itself, of being someone who handles money well. **Purpose** money in the service of something that actually matters to you, beyond the number. When your financial life is fueled by these rather than by comparison, something shifts: it stops being a race you can lose and becomes a craft you can improve.

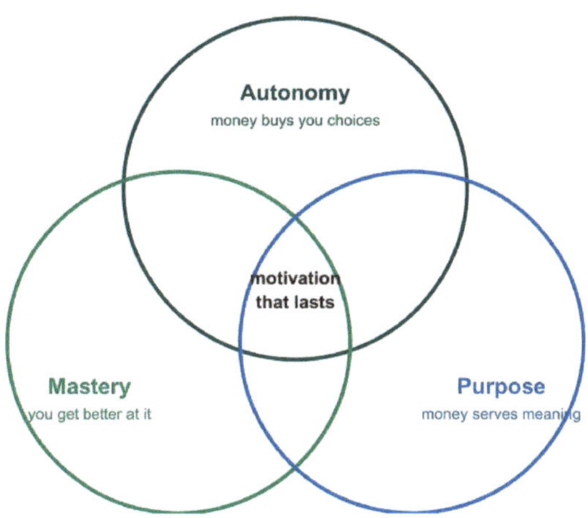

Durable motivation sits where autonomy, mastery, and purpose meet money as a source of choice, skill, and meaning rather than a scoreboard against other people.

This is also, quietly, what makes the difficult emotions easier to manage. Envy loses most of its grip when you're running your own race; status pressure fades when the point was never the signal. The inner work and the motivational work reinforce each other the more your money serves your own autonomy, mastery, and purpose, the less power the comparison-driven feelings have to hold the pen in the first place.

Feeling it without being driven by it

Put it all together and emotional agility is a single, learnable posture: feel the fear, name it, let the pause open, check it against what you actually value, and then choose. You don't have to be calm, calm is not the goal and often isn't available. You just have to be the one deciding, rather than the feeling. Like everything else in this book, it's a skill, not a trait, and it compounds: every time you let the pause open instead of acting on the impulse, the next time gets a little easier.

Consider Sofia, watching her investments drop sharply during a market panic, every headline screaming worse to come. The fear was real and physical the urge to sell everything and stop the pain was almost overwhelming. What she'd practiced wasn't suppressing the feeling but pausing inside it: naming it ("I'm terrified, and that's understandable"), then waiting before acting. She didn't pretend to be calm; she simply refused to let the panic hold the pen. She made no trade that week. The feeling passed, as feelings do; the market eventually recovered, as it has before; and the portfolio she didn't sell at the bottom stayed intact. Emotional agility didn't mean she felt no fear. It meant the fear got a vote, not a veto.

With that, the work of protection is complete. You've built the buffers that take the blow, a plan for the chaotic first weeks, a healthier relationship with your own mistakes, and a steadier hand when emotions run high. You can take a hit and recover and that resilience is what finally frees you to do more than survive. It lets you use your financial life to reach for something better. That's where the book turns next: to Grow.

Chapter summary

- Emotions are always present in money decisions and, in the hard moments, usually make them; financial agility rests on emotional agility.
- The common drivers fear, comparison, guilt, status, scarcity aren't irrational, but unmanaged they steer money toward worse outcomes.
- The tool isn't suppressing emotion but opening a pause: naming a feeling turns it from something driving you into something you can observe, letting your values decide.
- Extrinsic motivation (comparison, status, approval) is a treadmill that never satisfies; durable motivation comes from autonomy, mastery, and purpose.

Questions to think about

- Which emotion most often holds the pen in your money decisions fear, comparison, guilt, status, or scarcity?
- Think of a money decision you'd make differently with a 24-hour pause. What would the pause have changed?
- Is your financial drive mostly extrinsic (comparison, status) or intrinsic (autonomy, mastery, purpose)?
- What would "running your own race" with money actually look like for you?

Part Four · Grow: Turn Flexibility Into Opportunity

Everything so far has been, in a sense, defensive.

Part Two built room to move; Part Three made sure a shock couldn't take that room away. Both were about protecting your ability to keep going, no matter what the world did. This part is about something more ambitious: using that hard-won flexibility not just to survive what happens to you, but to reach for what could.

That requires rethinking what "growth" even means. The conventional picture of financial growth is a single number climbing a chart net worth, returns, the size of the pile. That picture isn't wrong, but in a world that keeps changing, it's dangerously incomplete. A large number reached by locking yourself onto one rigid path is far more fragile than a smaller one held by someone with options. Real growth the kind that survives a changing world isn’t only about accumulating more. It's about accumulating more *room to move*: more, and better, choices about what to do next.

There's a word for that, and it runs through this entire part: *optionality*. The central claim here is that in an uncertain world, optionality is the truest form of wealth. The person who is genuinely growing isn't just the one whose number is rising it’s the one whose range of possible futures is widening, who has more doors they could open, more directions they could turn, more chances they're positioned to take.

This is where the flexibility from the earlier parts finally pays off. Remember opportunity weather from Chapter Three: the rare chance that appears and rewards only those with the room to act on it. The breathing room, the diversified income, the buffers, the steadier emotions all of it was, in part, preparation for exactly these moments. Protection and growth turn out to be two sides of one coin. The same flexibility that lets you absorb a storm is what lets you seize a sunrise.

The four chapters ahead build this out. The first looks squarely at what wealth really is in a changing world, and makes the case that a good set of options is worth more than a bigger number. The second rethinks investing for a life that keeps moving how to grow your money without locking it up exactly when you might need it. The third turns to your single most valuable asset, your own earning power, and how to grow it so that you become more mobile, not less. And the fourth zooms out to the whole life: how to design one that keeps generating new moves rather than quietly closing them off.

A word on risk before we start, because "growth" is so often code for recklessness. Agile growth is not about betting bigger. It's about betting *better* making moves where the downside is small and known but the upside is open-ended, and refusing the reverse. The flexibility you built in the earlier parts is precisely what makes that kind of intelligent risk possible: you can afford to take a bet that might not pay off, because a bet that fails won't break you. Without that foundation, every risk is a gamble. With it, risk becomes something you can actually use.

So let's begin where growth begins in a world that won't sit still by looking honestly at what wealth is, and why the richest thing you can own is a good set of options.

Chapter 13 · Optionality Is the New Wealth

Imagine two people with the exact same net worth. The first has it all committed a home at the top of their budget, a single high-paying job their whole lifestyle depends on, money locked into things they can't easily touch. The second holds the same total far more loosely some in cash, skills that travel, a real network, very few hard commitments. On a statement, the two are identical. In life, they are not remotely equal, because one of them can move and the other can't.

This is the central idea of this part, and it cuts against how we usually keep score. We measure wealth as a number. But a number only tells you how much you *have* not how much you can *do* and in a world that keeps changing, what you can do is what actually matters. The truest measure of wealth isn't the size of the pile. It's the range of moves the pile makes available to you.

Optionality, defined

The idea comes from finance, where an *option* is the right, but not the obligation, to do something later you pay a little now for the freedom to choose once the future reveals itself. Optionality is simply having a lot of those: the standing capacity to act, or not, as conditions unfold. Cash is optionality. A portable skill is optionality. So is a warm relationship, a low-fixed-cost life, an unused line of credit. Each one is a door you've quietly kept the key to a future you could choose if you wanted to.

The shape of a good bet

The reason optionality compounds into real wealth comes down to a property called *convexity* the shape of how a bet can pay off. Some positions have a capped, known downside and an open-ended upside: the worst case is small and survivable, the best case is large and uncertain. Others are the exact reverse a small, capped upside sitting on top of a potentially catastrophic downside. (That second shape should sound familiar; it's the fragile debt from Chapter 8, and the all-in bet.) Agile growth means deliberately seeking the first shape and refusing the second.

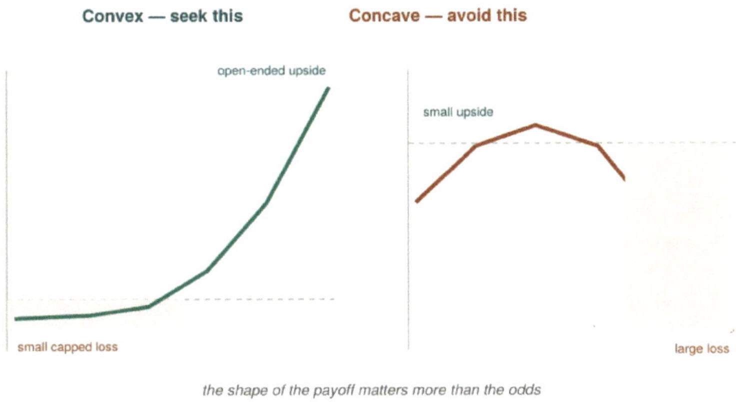

Two bets, two shapes. A convex bet risks a little for a lot; a concave bet risks a lot for a little. The shape of the payoff matters more than the odds.

Here's why this connects to flexibility. A convex bet you can comfortably afford to lose lets you keep taking swings and you only need a few to pay off. One big swing you *can't* afford to lose ends the game the first time it misses. Optionality the room you built in the earlier parts is precisely what lets you make convex bets at all, because it means a loss is survivable.

How optionality turns into moves

Optionality isn't an abstraction; it's made of concrete ingredients that combine to generate real choices. Cash on hand, current skills, a live network, and a low-lock-in life feed a kind of engine, and what comes out the other side is moves: take the deal, change direction, wait it out, say no, start something, relocate.

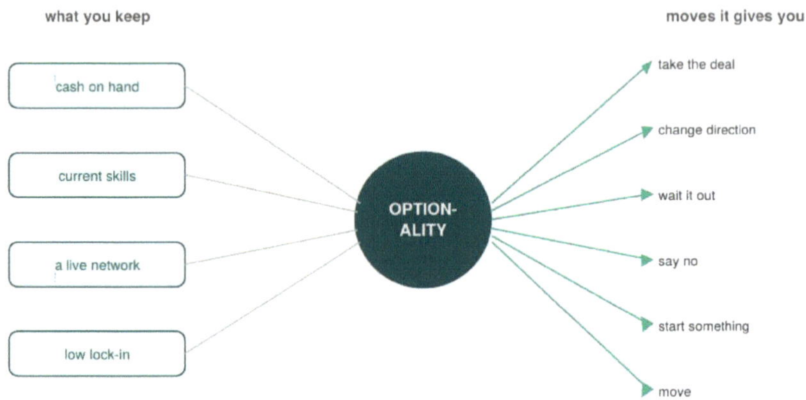

The optionality engine. A handful of things you keep cash, skills, relationships, low lock-in combine into a wide fan of moves you could make when the moment comes.

And it compounds. A move you make from a position of options tends to open new ones; a move you're *forced* into from a position of none tends to slam others shut. Optionality, used well, generates more optionality which is exactly the definition of growth this part is after.

Two kinds of rich

Which brings us back to our two people. By the number, they are equals. By optionality, they live in different worlds. It's worth being fair here: in a perfectly stable world, the locked-in one might even come out ahead, having left no "wasted" slack on the table. But we do not live in that world. In a changing one, the person with moves is wealthier in every sense that actually protects and grows a life.

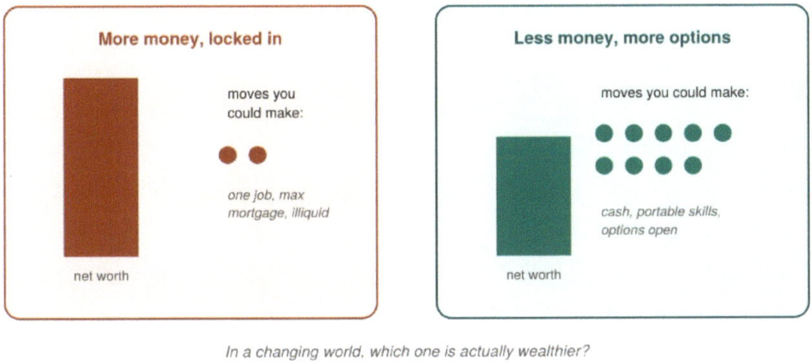

Same number on the statement, very different wealth. In a world that keeps changing, the moves you could make matter more than the size of the pile.

Buying optionality cheaply

The genuinely good news is that optionality is usually cheap, and often free. Keeping some dry powder, staying a learner, tending relationships before you need them, and refusing unnecessary lock-in cost very little and they pay off at exactly the moments that matter most, the opportunity weather of Chapter 3. That's the quiet magic of an option: the price to hold one is small, but the payoff when you finally get to exercise it can be enormous. You spend a little flexibility now to buy a lot of possibility later.

Consider Yusuf, who spent a few hundred dollars and a handful of weekends keeping a professional certification current in a field he no longer worked in. Friends teased him why maintain a door you're not walking through? For three years it looked like waste. Then his industry contracted sharply, and that dormant credential let him step sideways into an adjacent field within weeks, while colleagues scrambled to retrain from scratch. The cost of keeping the option open had been trivial; the payoff, when the weather turned, was enormous and lopsided. That's the shape of cheap optionality a small, certain, slightly annoying cost now, in exchange for a large, uncertain benefit later. You won't use most of the doors you keep open. You only need one of them to matter once.

Optionality is the lens for this entire part. The next three chapters make it concrete in how you invest, how you grow your own earning power, and how you design your life. We begin with money itself: how to grow it without locking it up at exactly the moment a moving life might need it most.

Chapter summary

- Two people with the same net worth can have wildly different wealth; the real measure is the range of moves your money makes available, not the size of the number.
- Optionality the right but not the obligation to act later is the truest form of wealth in a changing world; cash, portable skills, relationships, and a low-lock-in life are all optionality.
- Seek convex positions (small, capped downside, open-ended upside) and refuse concave ones; flexibility is what lets you make convex bets at all, because a loss stays survivable.
- Optionality compounds moves made from a position of options open new ones and it's usually cheap to buy: dry powder, learning, relationships, and refusing lock-in.

Questions to think about

- If you and someone with your exact net worth were compared by "moves available," who would look wealthier?
- Where in your finances do you have convexity capped downside, open upside and where do you have the dangerous reverse?
- What's one cheap option you could buy this year a skill, a relationship, some dry powder that might pay off big later?
- Which of your current commitments most reduces your optionality, and is the trade worth it?

Chapter 14 · Investing for a Moving Life

Most investing advice quietly assumes the straight-line life from Chapter One. It tells you to maximize long-term returns, stay fully invested, and not touch the money for thirty years advice that's excellent if your life never deviates from the plan. But a moving life deviates. Income wobbles, opportunities appear, emergencies land, and the money you "weren't going to touch for thirty years" turns out to be exactly the money you need now. Investing for a moving life means growing your money *without* locking it up at the precise moment you might need it.

Start with the real danger, because most people misidentify it. The danger isn't volatility markets rise and fall, and over decades the rises win. The danger is being *forced to sell at the wrong time.* A thirty-percent drop only becomes a permanent loss if you have to sell into it. The single most destructive thing a changing life does to an investment plan is force a sale at the bottom cashing out growth assets in a storm because there was nothing else to spend. Avoiding that one thing is most of the game.

Match the money to its timeline

The key question for any dollar you invest isn't "how do I maximize this?" It's "when will I need it?" Money you'll need soon has to be safe and reachable, even if that means accepting a lower return. Money you won't touch for many years can afford to ride out the swings in exchange for higher growth. Matching the asset to the horizon not chasing the highest return everywhere is the entire idea.

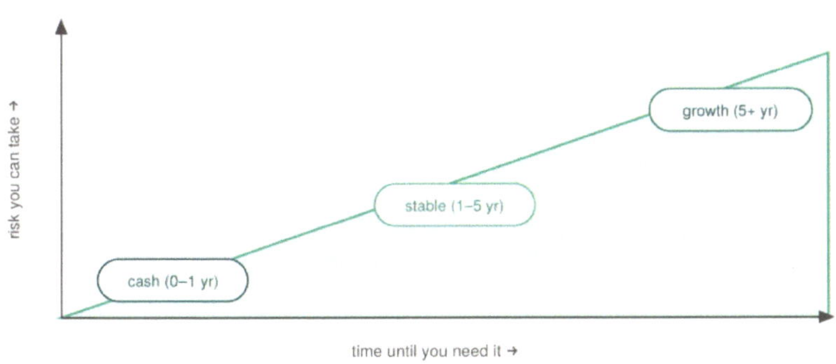

How much risk a dollar can take depends on how long until you need it. Short horizons demand safety and liquidity; long horizons can afford volatility in exchange for growth.

The three buckets

A simple structure builds this matching right in: divide your money into three buckets by when you'll need it. The **Now** bucket (zero to one year) is cash and equivalents the buffer from Chapter 9, fully liquid, no risk to principal. The **Soon** bucket (one to five years) holds steadier, lower-volatility assets for money with a known near-term purpose. The **Later** bucket (five years and beyond) holds the growth assets, the ones you can leave alone to compound and ride out the market's swings. Each bucket has a different job, so each one carries a different level of risk.

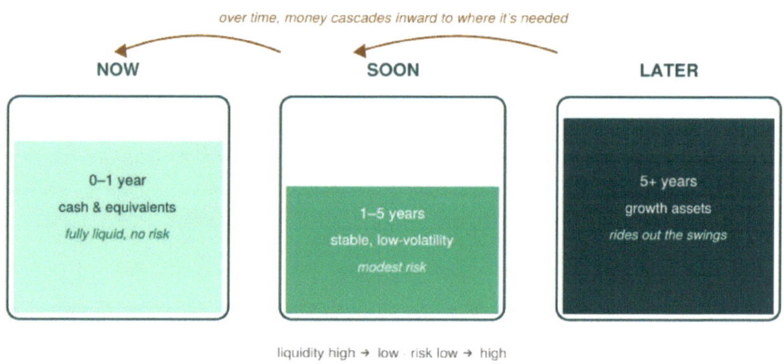

Three buckets, sorted by when you'll need the money. Liquidity falls and risk rises as you move from Now to Later and over time, money cascades inward toward where it's needed next.

Why buckets protect growth

The buckets aren't just tidy bookkeeping; they solve the forced-selling problem directly. When a storm hits, you spend from the Now bucket. You never have to reach into Later and sell growth assets at a low which means those assets get to do the one thing they actually need to do: stay invested through the dip and recover on the other side. The cash bucket is what buys the growth bucket the time it needs to work.

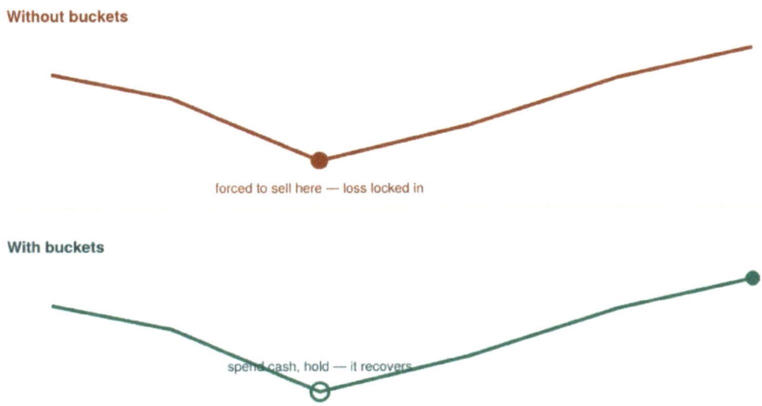

Same market dip, two outcomes. Without a cash bucket you sell at the bottom and lock in the loss; with one you spend cash, hold your growth assets, and let them recover.

Refilling, over time

This isn't set-and-forget; it flows. As time passes, money cascades inward the Later bucket refills Soon, and Soon refills Now so that money is always safe by the time it's needed and still growing while it isn't. In good years you top the buckets up; you rebalance occasionally; and after any storm, you refill the Now bucket first, exactly as you rebuilt your shock absorbers in Chapter 9.

Growth without the lock-in trap

The agile principle that ties it together: don't chase the absolute maximum return if the price is the flexibility to avoid selling at the bottom. A slightly lower expected return that you can actually hold through a storm beats a higher one that forces your hand at the worst moment. Liquidity, seen this way, is not the opposite of growth it's what allows growth to *survive* a moving life. And the reverse error is just as real: fleeing entirely into cash is its own kind of rigidity, one that quietly guarantees you fall behind. The buckets exist precisely to hold both truths at once.

Consider Mei, who did everything "right" on paper nearly all her money invested for maximum long-term growth. The flaw showed when she wanted to change careers and needed two years of living costs: her only option was to sell long-term holdings during a downturn, locking in losses to fund her present. After that, she organized by timeline instead of by one big number.

Near-term money she might need soon sat safe and reachable. Medium-term money took moderate risk. Only the genuinely long-term money chased growth, where time could ride out the dips. It looked less impressive than being “fully invested,” and it grew a touch slower. But it meant her plans never again forced her to raid her own future at the worst possible moment. The buckets protected the growth by protecting it from her own life.

Investing grows your money. But your single biggest engine of growth isn’t your portfolio it’s you. So we turn next to the most valuable asset you own: your own earning power, and how to grow it in a way that makes you more mobile, not less.

Chapter summary

- A moving life breaks the standard “invest and never touch it” advice; the goal is to grow money without locking it up exactly when you might need it.
- The real danger isn’t volatility but being forced to sell at the bottom; avoiding forced sales is most of the game.
- Match each dollar to its timeline money needed soon stays safe and liquid; money years away can ride out volatility for growth.
- The three buckets (Now, Soon, Later) build this in, so a storm is met from cash and your growth assets are never sold at a low; liquidity is what lets growth survive.

Questions to think about

- For your invested money, do you actually know when you’ll need each piece of it?
- If a storm hit, would you be forced to sell growth assets at a low or could you spend from cash and leave them alone?
- How many months sit in your “Now” bucket, and is your “Later” bucket truly money you can leave untouched for years?
- Where might chasing maximum return be quietly costing you the flexibility to hold through a downturn?

Chapter 15 · Career Growth and Skill Mobility

In Chapter Seven we treated your income like a portfolio to diversify. Now we go a step further, because your earning power isn't only an asset to protect it's the single highest-return investment most people will ever make, and the one most likely to be neglected. A modest, steady investment in your own skills compounds over a career into something that dwarfs almost any portfolio. The question this chapter answers is how to grow that asset so you become more *mobile* more able to move between roles, industries, and opportunities rather than more narrowly locked into one.

The trap of being the best at one thing

The conventional advice is to specialize: pick a lane and become the best in it. But being the single best at something is rare, and the strategy is surprisingly fragile. A lone skill can be automated, outsourced, or simply fall out of demand when the world shifts and a person built entirely around it has nowhere to go when it does. Worse, the pursuit of being "the best" locks you into one narrow lane for years. There is a more agile path, and it doesn't require being the best at anything.

Skill stacking

The idea, which the cartoonist Scott Adams put memorably, is this: you don't have to be the best at any one thing. Instead, get genuinely good not world-class, just good at a few complementary skills that add real value to you and to others, and combine them. The rare, valuable thing is the *combination.* A decent engineer who can also communicate clearly and has real design sense is far rarer, and far more valuable, than a slightly better engineer who can only engineer. Each skill you add doesn't just sum with the others; it multiplies, because it opens up new combinations that few other people can offer.

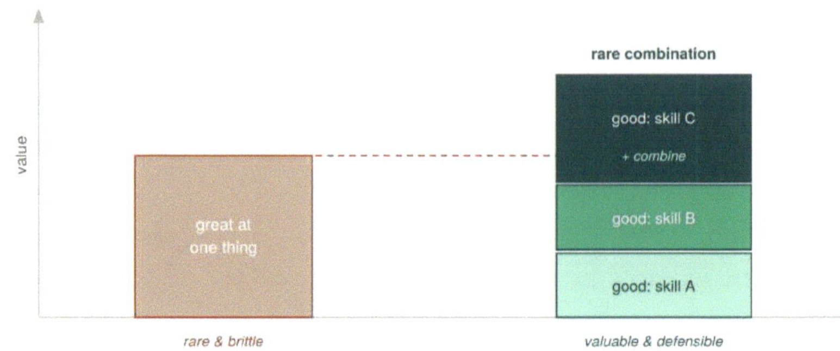

You don't have to be the best at one thing. A few good, complementary skills, combined, reach a value a single skill can't and the combination is far harder to replace.

Aim for a Pi (π)

A more modern shape to aim for is a **Pi (π)**. Picture the Greek letter: a broad bar across the top resting on *two* legs. The bar is breadth a working grasp of several adjacent skills, which gives you mobility. The two legs are *two* areas of genuine depth, each strong enough to be paid well for. This is what makes the Pi-shaped profile more resilient than the older T-shaped one, which stands on a single leg of depth. With two legs, a setback in one field doesn't topple you; you simply shift your weight onto the other and keep moving. The pure specialist is deep but brittle, balanced on one narrow point. The pure generalist is broad but has no leg to stand on at all. The Pi has both reach and two places to plant its feet.

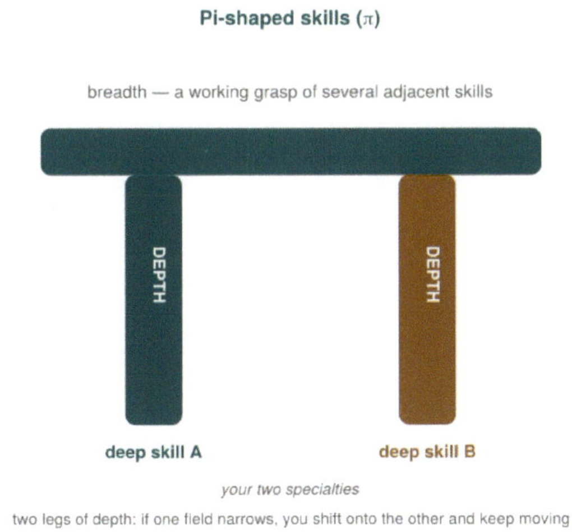

The Pi-shaped (π) profile: two legs of real depth under a broad bar of breadth. Two specialties mean that if one field narrows, you shift onto the other instead of falling.

Build for transfer

Within all this, prize the skills that *transfer*. Some abilities travel across nearly any industry clear communication, sound judgment, problem-solving, selling, the ability to learn quickly, basic comfort with data and technology. These are mobility insurance. When one industry contracts, transferable skills let you carry your value into another rather than starting from zero. Role-specific skills earn you money now; transferable skills are what keep earning when the specific role disappears. A career built on both is far harder to strand.

Skills compound and they decay

Two facts about skills sit in tension, and holding both is the whole game. Skills *compound:* each one makes the next easier to learn and more valuable in combination, so a steady learner pulls away from a stagnant one over time. But skills also *decay:* their useful half-life is shrinking as the world changes faster, so a skill you stop maintaining quietly loses value whether you notice or not. The response is the one this whole book keeps returning to small, continuous investment in normal weather. A little learning, sustained, beats the occasional panicked crash-course every time. Put another way, every skill has a shelf life. Some judgments, communication, selling, the ability to learn have decades of runway ahead of them; others are already near their expiry as tools and platforms turn over. The agile move is to pour most of your investment into the long-shelf-life skills, keep a working familiarity with the rest, and let the ones with no future quietly lapse rather than clinging to them out of sunk-cost pride.

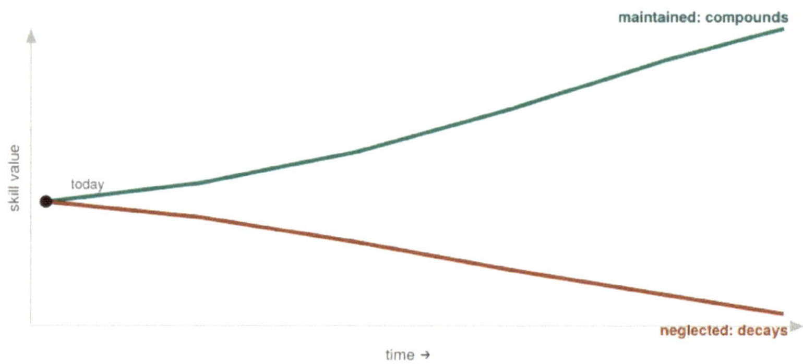

The same skill, two paths. Maintained and built on, it compounds; left alone, it quietly decays which is why steady, ordinary learning matters more than heroic bursts.

Treat learning as a position

Tie it back to the idea that runs through this part: every skill you add is a cheap *option* on your own future. It costs a little now some time, some effort and it might pay off enormously if the world turns toward it, while costing little if it doesn't. You don't have to predict which skill will be the one that matters; a well-built stack is a portfolio of options on yourself, and you only need a few of them to pay off. Invest in your own capabilities the way you'd build any convex position: many small, affordable bets with open-ended upside.

Consider Grace, who treated her skills the way an investor treats holdings reviewing them, not just accumulating them. She had real depth in two areas (her Pi's two legs) plus a working grasp of several adjacent ones. Each year she asked a blunt question of each skill: does this still have shelf life, or is it quietly expiring? When a software tool she'd mastered was clearly being superseded, she didn't cling to it out of sunk-cost pride she let it go and redirected that learning time toward a skill with a long runway ahead. She wasn't learning more than her peers. She was curating better: adding skills that added value, deepening her two legs, and deliberately discarding the ones whose shelf life had run out. Her capability stayed current because she managed it like a portfolio, not a trophy shelf.

Skills make you mobile within your working life. The final chapter of this part zooms all the way out to the whole life and asks how to design one that keeps generating new moves instead of quietly closing them off.

Chapter summary

- Your earning power is the highest-return investment you can make, and the goal is to grow it toward mobility, not narrow lock-in.
- Skill stacking beats being the best at one thing: a rare combination of a few good, complementary skills is more valuable and more defensible than a single elite skill.
- Aim for a Pi (π) *two* areas of real depth under a broad bar of breadth, so that if one field narrows you can shift onto the other; and prize transferable skills that travel across industries.
- Skills both compound and decay, so invest continuously in normal weather; each new skill is a cheap option on your own future.

Questions to think about

- What two or three skills could you combine into a rarer, more valuable stack than any one of them alone?
- Are you a brittle one-legged specialist, a shallow generalist, or building a Pi (π) with two solid legs and which second area of depth would most strengthen you?
- Which of your skills are transferable across industries, and which would vanish if your industry did?
- What's one small, consistent learning habit you could actually sustain in normal weather?

Chapter 16 · Designing a Life with More Moves

We've grown optionality in your money, your investments, and your skills. This final chapter of the part pulls back to the widest view the whole shape of a life and asks the question sitting underneath all financial planning: how do you plan for a future you can't predict? The honest answer is that you don't plan it the old way. You design a life that keeps generating moves, and you steer it with a different kind of plan.

The two bad answers

There are two common responses to an uncertain future, and both fail. The first is the rigid long-term plan the detailed, fixed, thirty-year blueprint that feels reassuring and goes quietly obsolete the moment life deviates from it, which, as Chapter One argued, it always does. The second is the opposite: no plan at all, pure drift, reacting to whatever shows up and ending up nowhere in particular. One is a map that stops matching the territory; the other is no map at all. The agile path is a third thing.

A direction, not a route

Borrow again from how good teams handle deep uncertainty: commit to a *direction*, not a fixed route. Set a north star a clear sense of where you're trying to go, rooted in the values you named in Chapter Four and then take short, adaptive steps toward it, re-checking and re-planning as you learn and as the ground shifts. The destination holds steady; the path is allowed to flex. You can change almost everything about *how* you get there without ever losing the *where.*

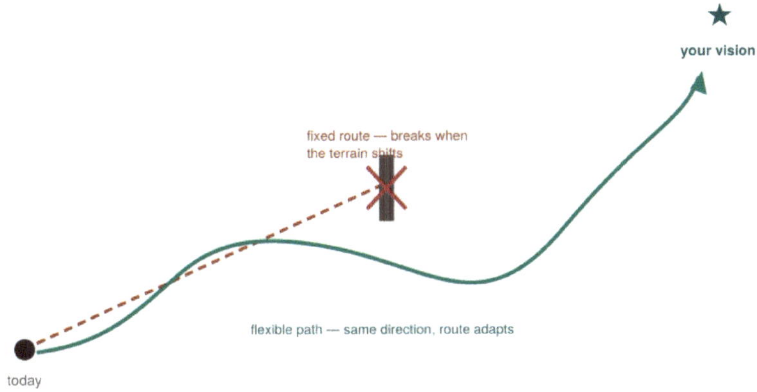

A fixed route breaks the moment the terrain changes. A flexible path keeps the same direction the same north star while adapting the route around whatever appears.

Plan short, inside a long vision

In practice this means holding two horizons at once. The long vision years or decades out is held loosely, as a direction rather than a schedule. The short plan a season, a quarter is held firmly enough to act on but loosely enough to revise. You don't try to plan year seven in detail; you plan the next short stretch well, take it, see what you learned, and plan the next one from where you actually are. It's the same adaptive cadence underneath agile work, applied to a whole life and it previews the reflection loop we'll build in the final part.

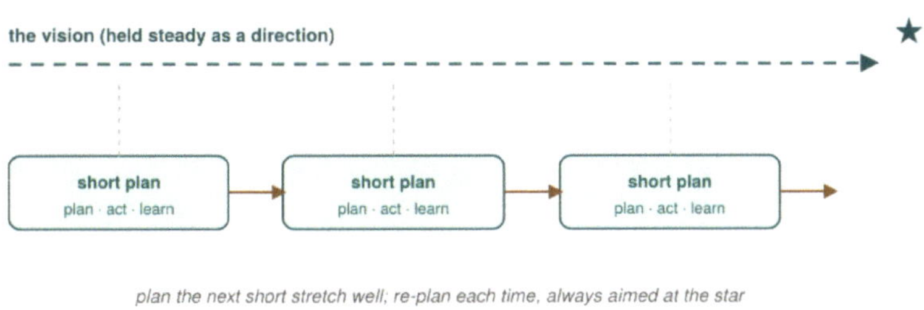

Hold the vision steady as a direction, then plan in short, revisable stretches each one acted on, learned from, and re-planned, always aimed at the same star.

Design choices that add moves

Here is where it gets practical and ties the whole part together. Every major life decision where you live, what you commit to, what you buy, what you bind yourself to either *adds* future moves or *removes* them. A flexible choice keeps your options open; a lock-in choice prunes them. The agile move is to favor decisions that preserve optionality whenever the cost of doing so is low: renting over a stretch purchase when you're genuinely unsure, work and skills that travel, geographic and remote flexibility, reversible commitments over irreversible ones, leaving a little slack rather than filling every gap. It's the Chapter 8 flexibility test and the Chapter 13 optionality lens, applied to life rather than just money.

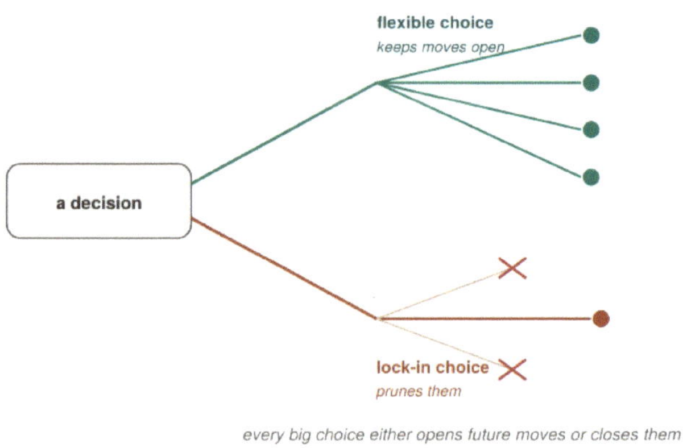

Every big decision either opens future moves or prunes them. Favor the choices that keep your options open especially when keeping them open is cheap.

This is emphatically *not* an argument against commitment. Some commitments to people, to a calling, to a place you love are worth their cost in flexibility many times over, and you should make them gladly. The point is narrower and more useful: don't surrender your moves *by accident*, trading away flexibility for things that don't actually matter to you. Spend it on purpose, on what you truly value, and keep it everywhere else.

The compounding of a flexible life

Just as optionality compounds in money and in skills, it compounds across a whole life. Each flexible choice keeps the next set of choices open; each one keeps you positioned to catch the opportunity weather when it comes. A life designed this way doesn't merely survive change it becomes *more* possible over time, not less, as options stack on options. That is what growth means in the agile sense: not just a bigger number at the end, but a wider, more open future the whole way through.

Consider the Okafor household, who made one quietly radical decision a decade ago: they'd optimize their life for moves, not for status. They kept fixed costs deliberately low even as income rose, stayed renters longer than friends thought wise, and kept skills and savings portable. Year to year it looked unremarkable, even over-cautious. But each flexible choice compounded with the others. Low fixed costs made a career risk affordable; the career risk led to better work; better work funded more options; more options made the next bold move easier still. A friend who'd locked into a big mortgage and a single career path watched the Okafors take chances she couldn't. They weren't luckier or higher-earning. They'd simply spent ten years stacking small flexibilities and flexibility, like money, compounds.

And with that, we've now built the entire agile financial life in miniature one that adapts in calm weather, protects against storms, and grows by widening its options. But there are moments when change isn't weather at all. It's a genuine turning point: a marriage, a child, a move, a new career, a retirement. These big transitions test everything we've built, all at once, and they deserve a part of their own. That's where we go next.

Chapter summary

- Planning for an unpredictable future means designing a life that keeps generating moves not locking in a fixed long-term plan, and not drifting with no plan at all.
- Commit to a direction, not a route: hold a values-based vision steady while taking short, adaptive steps and re-planning as you learn.
- Every major life decision adds or removes future moves; favor choices that preserve optionality when the cost is low, and spend flexibility deliberately, not by accident.
- Optionality compounds in a life as in money and skills a flexible life becomes more possible over time, which is what growth means in a changing world.

Questions to think about

- What's your north star the direction you're steering toward stated clearly enough to guide a real decision?
- Where are you running a rigid long-term plan that life has already outdated, or drifting with no direction at all?
- Which recent or upcoming decision adds future moves, and which quietly removes them?
- Where are you giving up flexibility by accident, for something that doesn't actually matter to you?

Part Five · Bending Through Life's Big Transitions

Most of this book has been about ongoing conditions the everyday weather of a financial life, and how to adapt, protect, and grow through it. But some changes aren't weather at all. They're turning points: a partnership, a child, a move, a new career, the slow shift into retirement. They don't pass like a storm; they permanently reshape the landscape. And they have a way of testing everything you've built, all at once.

These are the transitions the "transition weather" we named back in Chapter Three. What sets them apart is that they're usually at least partly chosen, and they're foreseeable: you can often see them coming, even if you can't say exactly when. That visibility is a gift, because it means transitions reward the one thing this book keeps returning to deliberate redesign, done *before* the change locks in, rather than a scramble afterward.

The real danger of a big transition isn't the change itself. It's the rigidity the change quietly installs while you're not looking. Each one tends to bolt on fixed costs, new commitments, and assumptions that harden into your "normal" before you've ever examined them. A wedding becomes a mortgage becomes a school district becomes a career you can no longer afford to leave. Handled passively, transitions are where flexibility goes to die every one adding another weight to a life with less and less give. Handled deliberately, they are the exact opposite: the best possible moments to rebuild flexibility on purpose, precisely because you're already rearranging everything anyway. A transition is the rare moment when the whole structure is in motion and can be re-engineered.

This part takes the three transitions that reshape most financial lives. The first is family what happens when money stops being yours alone and becomes a shared, negotiated thing between you and the people you love. The second is housing and place the largest fixed cost and the heaviest lock-in most people ever take on, alongside the geographic flexibility almost no one fully uses. The third is retirement, which we'll treat not as a finish line with a single magic number, but as a design problem to be solved flexibly, with many levers rather than one.

In each, the approach is the same, and you already hold the tools. Bring the manifesto your values, now sometimes shared with someone else. Protect the breathing room. Run the flexibility test on the big commitments. Favor the choices that keep your options open. A transition, in the end, is just a concentrated dose of everything the book has taught: a single moment when adapting, protecting, and growing all come due together.

So let's begin with the transition that changes money most profoundly of all the moment it stops being a solo endeavor.

Chapter 17 · Family Money

Money is never just math. By the time you're an adult, your relationship with it has been shaped by decades of history how you grew up, what you feared, what you saw modeled, what scarcity or plenty quietly taught you. It is personal, and largely invisible, even to yourself. And then, at some point, it stops being yours alone. You partner with someone. You have children. You begin caring for a parent. Money becomes a *we* and that shift reshapes a financial life more profoundly than almost any other transition in this book.

Two money stories, merging

When two people combine their finances, the spreadsheet makes it look simple: add the incomes, add the expenses, share the total. But underneath, they're merging two entire money histories two sets of values, habits, fears, and unspoken assumptions about what money is even *for*, formed long before the two of them ever met. That's the real merger, and it's why combining finances so often produces friction that the numbers alone could never explain.

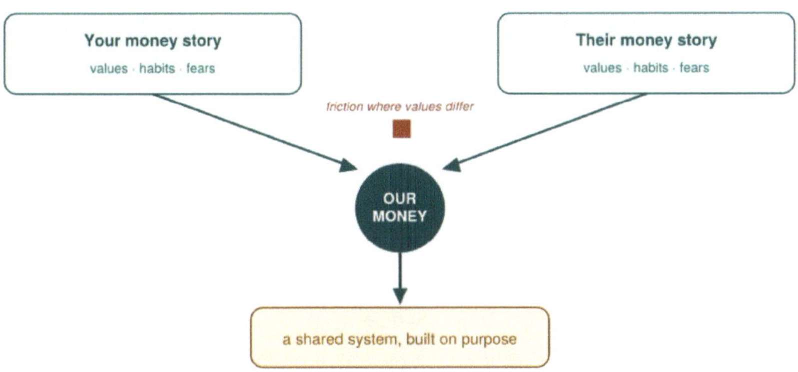

Combining finances merges two whole money histories, not just two budgets and the friction shows up exactly where the underlying values differ.

Why money fights aren't about money

Here is the single most useful thing to understand about money and the people you love: most money conflict is not a disagreement about a purchase. It's a collision of values that neither person has named out loud. One partner says “let’s save more” and means *prudence;* the other hears *you don’t trust me to enjoy life.* The argument on the surface is about the new couch. The real subject underwater, unspoken is security versus freedom, or control, or a childhood memory of going without.

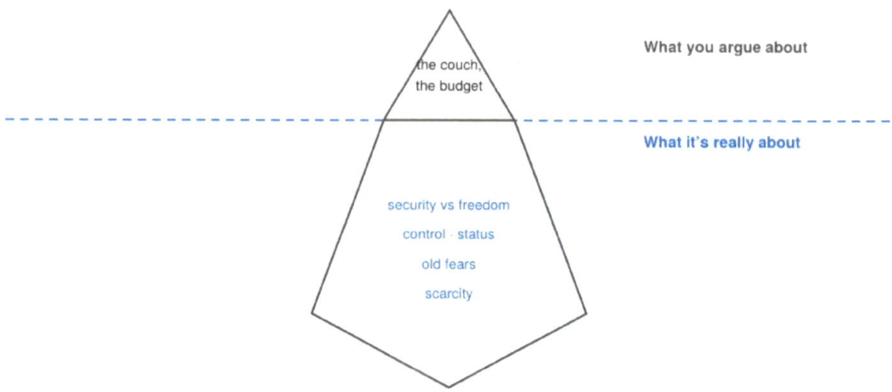

The thing you argue about is the visible tip. The thing it’s really about the values and old fears beneath the surface is the far larger mass underwater.

This changes what a fix even looks like. If the conflict were really about the couch, a better spreadsheet would solve it. But it isn’t, so it won’t. The only thing that resolves it is bringing the underwater part to the surface naming the values underneath, where the real, and genuinely resolvable, difference actually lives.

A shared manifesto

This is where the manifesto from Chapter 4 grows up into a *we.* The most valuable thing a couple or family can do is not to agree on every number that’s neither possible nor necessary. It’s to agree on a few shared values, a shared manifesto, and to build a habit of talking about money before it becomes a crisis. Once you’ve jointly decided that “we value breathing room over the biggest house,” the couch argument suddenly has a reference point that isn’t simply whose turn it is to win.

Money working agreements you can renegotiate

Just as important: make your money working agreements *renegotiable.* Who earns, who pays for what, how you split things, how you'll handle a windfall or a shock set these as living agreements you revisit at each turn, not as once-and-forever rules carved at the start. Life will keep changing the inputs: a baby, a job loss, a raise, a move, an illness. An agreement that can't flex with those changes doesn't hold the relationship steady; it slowly becomes a source of resentment. So revisit on purpose, in calm weather, the same way you revisit everything else in this book.

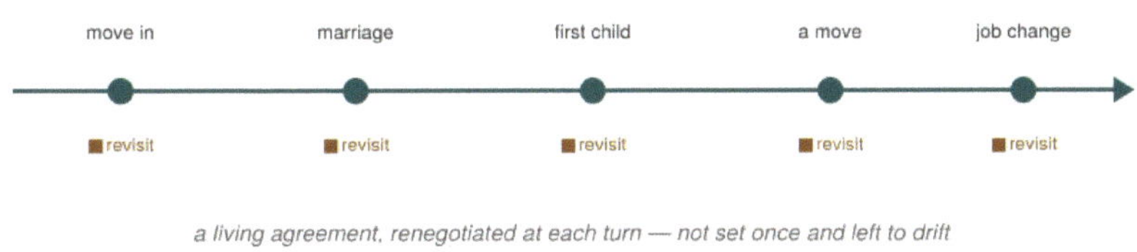

Treat the money agreement as living. Revisit it deliberately at each turning point, rather than setting it once and letting it quietly drift out of date.

Children: meaning, and rigidity

Children are among the most profound sources of meaning a life can hold and, financially, one of its most significant sources of rigidity. They add large, long-lasting, hard-to-reduce fixed costs, and they shrink your slack at exactly the stage when a stable income feels most necessary. The agile response isn't to flinch from the commitment; it's to go in clear-eyed. Protect the breathing room fiercely, because it now belongs to everyone. Resist stacking every optional expense on top of an already-larger fixed base. And over time, model and teach flexibility to them, because the most valuable thing you can pass on isn't a sum of money it's the capacity to bend.

The other direction: aging parents

Transitions also run upward. Caring for aging parents financially, practically, emotionally is an increasingly common transition, and one that tends to arrive partly foreseeable and partly all at once. It rewards the very same moves: the hard, invaluable conversations held in advance; buffers built in anticipation rather than panic; and shared agreements among siblings reached before the pressure hits, not during it. For those caught in the middle supporting children and parents at the same time the breathing room you protected in the earlier parts is precisely what keeps the whole arrangement from breaking.

Consider Daniel and his two siblings, who discovered their mother needed expensive ongoing care and had no plan for it. The first months were chaos money flowing unevenly, one sibling quietly resentful at carrying more, no one saying the hard things aloud. What rescued them wasn't more money; it was treating the situation as a shared, renegotiable agreement. They sat down together, put the real numbers on the table, and agreed openly who would contribute what in money, in time, in logistics given each one's very different circumstances. They wrote it down and agreed to revisit it every few months as things changed. The arrangement wasn't perfectly equal, because their situations weren't. But because it was explicit and could flex, it held. The fight had never really been about money. It was about fairness left unspoken.

Family is the transition that changes money most deeply, because it changes whose money it even is. The next one changes where your money is anchored and takes on the single largest fixed cost most people ever carry.

Chapter summary

- Money becomes a "we" at major transitions partnering, children, aging parents merging two whole money histories, not just two budgets.
- Most money conflict is a collision of unspoken values (security vs freedom, control, old fears), not a disagreement about numbers; the argument is the tip, the values are the iceberg.
- A shared manifesto a few agreed values plus a habit of talking about money resolves more than any spreadsheet, because it addresses the real difference.
- Make money agreements renegotiable and revisit them at each turn; protect breathing room as children and aging parents add fixed costs and shrink slack.

Questions to think about

- What's your own "money story" and do the people you share money with actually know it?
- The last money argument you had: what was the surface topic, and what value was really underneath?
- Do you and your partner or family have a shared manifesto and a regular time to talk money or only crisis conversations?
- Which of your money agreements have gone unrevisited even though the inputs have clearly changed?

Chapter 18 · Housing, Relocation, and Geographic Flexibility

No single decision shapes a financial life as much as where and how you live. Housing is almost always the largest line in the budget, the biggest fixed cost, and the heaviest commitment most people ever take on. It sets the floor under your spending, determines how much breathing room is left above, and because it ties you to a place quietly governs how mobile you can be. Get housing right and a great deal of the rest gets easier. Get it wrong and it can lock a whole life in place for years.

The master fixed cost

Housing isn't just an expense; it's the expense that determines all the others. A too-large housing cost compresses everything beneath it less breathing room from Chapter 5, less room for spending to contract from Chapter 6, less ability to absorb a shock or chase an opportunity. It is the single biggest lever most people have over their own flexibility, which means the single most powerful move available to most people is also the most boring one: keep housing costs comfortably below what you could technically "afford."

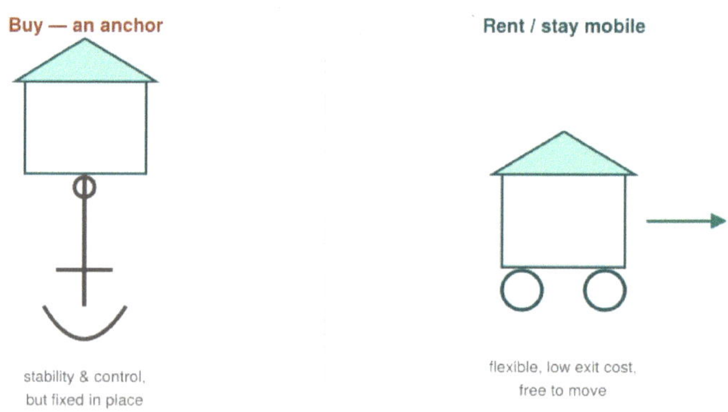

Housing is the floor everything else sits on. Right-sized, it leaves real breathing room above; oversized, it quietly squeezes that room down to nothing.

Rent versus buy, reframed

The usual debate is a trap. "Renting is throwing money away" versus "buying builds wealth" both slogans miss the point, because the real question was never purely financial. It's a question about flexibility. Buying is an *anchor:*

it offers stability, control, a kind of forced saving, and a hedge against rising rents but it's also a large, concentrated, illiquid bet that's expensive and slow to exit and ties you to one location. Renting is *mobility:* flexibility, no transaction cost to move, easy to adjust but no equity and less control. Neither is simply "right." Each one buys a genuinely different thing.

Buying and renting aren't better and worse they're an anchor and mobility. One buys stability and control; the other buys the freedom to move.

So the question becomes refreshingly concrete: how much flexibility does your life actually need right now? Early in a career, in an uncertain industry, in an evolving relationship, unsure of where you'll even want to be flexibility is worth a great deal, and renting buys it cheaply. Settled, rooted, clear on your place and your plans an anchor can be exactly right, and its lock-in becomes a feature rather than a flaw. Match the housing to your weather, just as you matched everything else in Chapter 3.

The over-anchor trap

The most common and most costly housing mistake isn't renting for too long. It's anchoring too heavily, too soon buying at the very top of the budget, in a place the life hasn't actually settled on yet. That single move takes the largest, least reversible decision available to you and turns it into a flexibility sink, exactly the rigid, hard-to-exit commitment the Chapter 8 flexibility test warns against. (It's the same "biggest house I could afford" that the regret in Chapter 11 was built on.) A home you love that still leaves you room to move will almost always serve you better than a larger one that doesn't.

Geographic flexibility as optionality

Where you live is itself an option, and it's one most people never exercise. Cost of living, job markets, taxes, and opportunities vary enormously from place to place. The ability and willingness to move amplified now by the remote-capable skills from Chapter 15 is a powerful and badly underused form of optionality. It widens the set of opportunities you can reach and the storms you can step out of the way of. You don't have to actually move for this to be valuable; as with every option, the worth is in being *able* to.

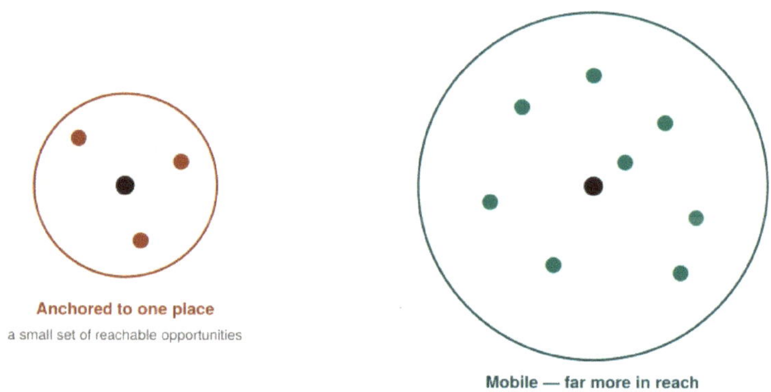

Geographic mobility widens your reach. Anchored, you can only act on what's nearby; mobile, far more opportunities fall inside the circle of what you could actually take.

Designing housing for your weather

There is, in the end, no universal answer here only a fit. In high-change seasons of life, weight flexibility: rent, stay light, keep your mobility intact. In settled seasons, an anchor can be a genuine and lasting good. And like every transition in this part, housing rewards revisiting: the right arrangement for one chapter of life is frequently wrong for the next, and the willingness to re-decide to sell, to move, to resize is itself a form of the flexibility this whole book is about. Choose your housing deliberately, for the weather you're actually in, rather than defaulting into the heaviest anchor you can lift.

Consider Tariq, who moved to a new city for a promising but uncertain job. Everyone urged him to buy immediately "renting is throwing money away." He read his own weather instead: new role, new city, a future he couldn't yet predict. So he rented deliberately for two years, staying light and mobile, paying a premium he thought of as buying optionality. The job turned out to be wrong for him; because he rented, leaving cost him a month's notice, not a forced sale in a market he didn't understand. When he later landed somewhere he genuinely wanted to stay, he bought anchoring himself on purpose, with eyes open. Housing wasn't a one-size rule for him. It was a choice he matched to the weather he was actually in.

Housing anchors your money in a place. The last transition in this part concerns where all of it is ultimately heading and asks us to treat retirement not as a finish line, but as a design problem.

Chapter summary

- Housing is the master fixed cost it sets your breathing room, spending floor, and mobility; keeping it well below what you "could afford" is the single biggest flexibility move.
- Rent vs buy isn't mainly financial; it's a flexibility trade buying is an anchor, renting is mobility and the right choice depends on how much flexibility your life needs now.
- The common mistake is over-anchoring too soon: buying at the top of budget before life has settled turns the biggest decision into a flexibility sink.
- Geographic mobility, amplified by remote skills, is a powerful and underused form of optionality the value is in being able to move, not in moving.

Questions to think about

- What share of your income goes to housing and how much breathing room would you gain by lowering it?
- Does your current housing fit your weather flexibility for a high-change season, or an anchor for a settled one?
- If a great opportunity appeared in another city, how easily could you actually take it?
- Are you anchored more heavily than your life is actually settled?

Chapter 19 · Retirement as a Design Problem

Retirement, as it's conventionally sold, is built around two rigid ideas: a number and a date. Save until you hit the magic number, then on the chosen date step off the cliff from full-time work to no work, all at once and live off the pile for the rest of your life. It's a clean story, and it's also one of the most fragile financial plans a person can make, because it asks you to predict the unpredictable: market returns, your health, your lifespan, and your own desires, decades in advance.

Why the fixed finish line is fragile

The single-number, single-date model concentrates an enormous amount of uncertainty onto one moment and one bet. Retire just before a market downturn and the very number that was "enough" suddenly isn't. Live longer than you planned for and a pile sized for twenty-five years has to stretch across thirty-five. A serious health event rewrites everything. Against any of this, a single rigid plan has no real response except hope and hope is not a strategy for the last third of your life.

Retirement as a design problem

The agile reframe is to stop treating retirement as a finish line and start treating it as a *design problem* and design problems have multiple levers, never just one. Instead of betting everything on a single number reached on a single date, you build a flexible system with several controls you can adjust. And here is the property that makes it work: flexibility on any one lever takes pressure off all the others. You don't need to have predicted the perfect number if you can adjust the timing, the spending, or the work as you go.

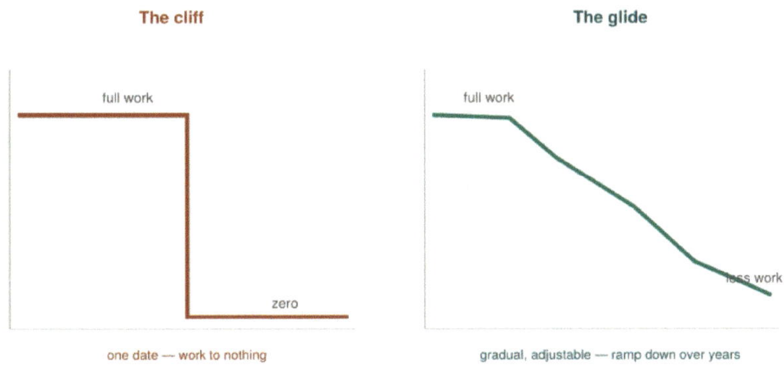

The conventional retirement is a cliff full work to nothing, on one date. A more agile version is a glide: a gradual, adjustable ramp you can steer as conditions change.

The levers

The controls you can design around are more numerous than most people realize. **Timing** shifting the transition even by a year or two changes the math dramatically. **Spending** a level that can flex downward in bad years rather than staying fixed. **Work** keeping some income rather than stopping cold. **Withdrawals** flexible drawdowns instead of a rigid fixed amount. And **buffers** cash to ride out bad early years, exactly as in Chapters 9 and 14. A retirement that can move on several of these at once is robust in a way that no single perfect number ever could be.

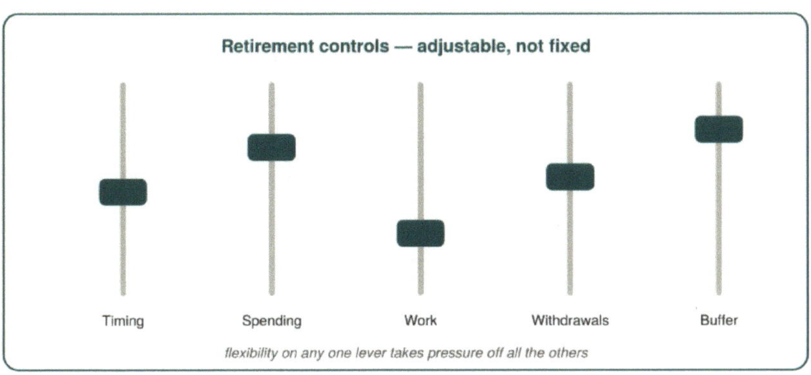

Retirement has many levers, not one. Because flexibility on any single control eases the pressure on the rest, you don't need to get the number exactly right.

Sequence risk and flexible spending

The most dangerous stretch in a retirement is the few years right around the transition. A bad market early while you've just started drawing money out does lasting damage, because you're selling into the dip exactly as Chapter 14 warned. The defenses are the same agile ones we've used throughout: a cash bucket so you're not forced to sell low, and a spending level that can flex down for a year or two when needed. Fixed withdrawals into a falling market drain the tank alarmingly fast; spending that can give a little makes the same tank last.

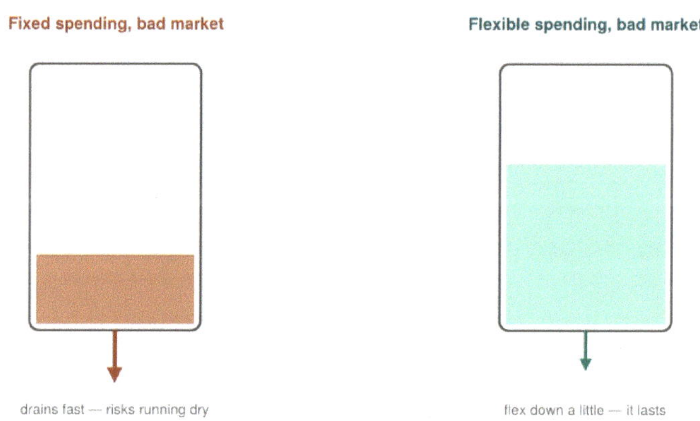

Into a bad early market, fixed spending drains the tank fast and risks running dry; flexing spending down even a little is often what makes it last.

Work optional, not work over

The hard full-stop is also giving way to something more flexible, and often simply better: phased or partial retirement "work optional" rather than "work over." Keeping some engagement, whether part-time, consulting, or a passion that happens to pay, does several things at once. It adds income, it adds optionality, it supplies the autonomy, mastery, and purpose from Chapter 12 and it lowers the number you needed to accumulate in the first place. Retirement, seen this way, isn't a single day you stop. It's a gradual reshaping of how, and how much, you work.

A living plan

Finally, a retirement plan is not something you set once at forty and execute unchanged at sixty-five. It's revisited as markets, health, and your own desires reveal themselves, with the levers adjusted along the way. That makes it the perfect bridge to the final part of this book because adjusting as you go isn't a one-time act of planning. It's a *practice.*

Consider Anika, who'd always pictured retirement as a hard cliff full-time at 64, fully stopped at 65. As it approached, the cliff felt both frightening and unnecessary, so she redesigned it as a glide instead of a drop. She shifted to three days a week at 63, kept a small consulting thread for two years after "retiring," and treated her plan as a living document she revisited yearly rather than a fixed finish line. When markets dipped early on, she simply dialed her spending and her consulting up and down a little instead of panicking the flexibility absorbed the shock. Her retirement wasn't a single date she had to get exactly right. It was a set of adjustable levers she kept her hands on, and that was what made it feel safe.

The big transitions family, home, and retirement all reward the same things: bringing your values, protecting your room, and redesigning deliberately instead of defaulting. But doing that consistently, across a whole life, takes more than understanding it once. It takes a practice you can actually keep. That is the final part of the book.

Chapter summary

- The conventional retirement one number, one date, a hard stop is fragile because it asks you to predict markets, health, and lifespan decades ahead.
- Treat retirement as a design problem with multiple adjustable levers timing, spending, work, withdrawals, buffers where flexibility on any one lever relieves pressure on the others.
- Sequence risk near the transition is the key danger; a cash buffer and flexible (not fixed) spending protect you from selling into an early downturn.
- "Work optional" rather than "work over" adds income, optionality, and purpose while lowering the number you need and the plan should be revisited and adjusted as life unfolds.

Questions to think about

- Is your retirement plan a single number and date or a flexible design with several levers you could adjust?
- If a market downturn hit in your first years of retirement, what would you adjust and have you planned for it?
- Could you flex your spending down for a year or two without crisis if you needed to?
- What might "work optional" look like for you and how would it change the number you need?

Part Six · The Built to Bend Practice

By now you have the whole picture. You know how to adapt in ordinary weather, protect against storms, grow by widening your options, and bend through life's big transitions. You have the concepts and the tools. And if this book stopped right here, most of it would slowly stop working not because the ideas are wrong, but because ideas, left alone, decay. Good intentions fade. The lifestyle ratchet creeps back. Last year's plan quietly stops matching this year's life. Understanding something once is simply not the same as living it.

The difference between people who stay financially agile and people who read a book like this and change nothing is almost never knowledge. It's practice a light, repeatable rhythm that keeps the ideas alive and adjusting. This is the secret hiding in plain sight in how agile teams actually work. They don't just hold good principles in their heads; they run regular, lightweight routines short cycles of planning, doing, reviewing, and improving that turn principles into habits and habits into results. The principles are the easy part. The cadence is what makes them real.

This final part hands you the personal version of that cadence: a practice for a financial life that's built to bend. It has four simple moving parts, and a closing chapter to tie everything together. First, a scorecard that lets you actually measure your flexibility, rather than just your wealth. Then timeboxing and money sprints, to make change happen instead of merely intending it. Then a reflection loop, to keep improving on purpose rather than by accident. And then coaching yourself forward staying accountable and kind to yourself at the same time, which turns out to be harder and more important than it sounds.

One warning, and it matters more than it might seem. The practice itself has to stay flexible. It would be a strange failure to take a book about avoiding rigidity and turn it into one more rigid system that runs your life. So everything here is deliberately light minutes, not hours; a rhythm, not a regime. The goal is a practice you'll actually keep, because a sustainable light practice beats an ambitious one you abandon within a month. If any of it ever starts to feel like a cage, you're doing it wrong, and the right response is to loosen it.

So here is the last move: turning everything you now understand into something you actually do quietly, repeatedly, for the rest of your life. We begin by learning to measure the one thing this entire book has been about how much your money can bend.

Chapter 20 · The Bend Scorecard

There's an old line in management: you can't manage what you don't measure. The trouble is that the usual financial metrics net worth, income, savings rate all measure the *size* of your money, not its flexibility. They tell you how much you have, not how well it can bend. This whole book has argued that flexibility is what actually protects and grows a life in a changing world, so the practice has to begin by measuring that. You need a scorecard for bend.

Here's a simple one. Four dimensions, easy to remember because together they spell the very thing they give you: **M.O.V.E.** Maneuver room, Optionality, Velocity, and Exposure. Between them, they capture how much room your financial life actually has to move.

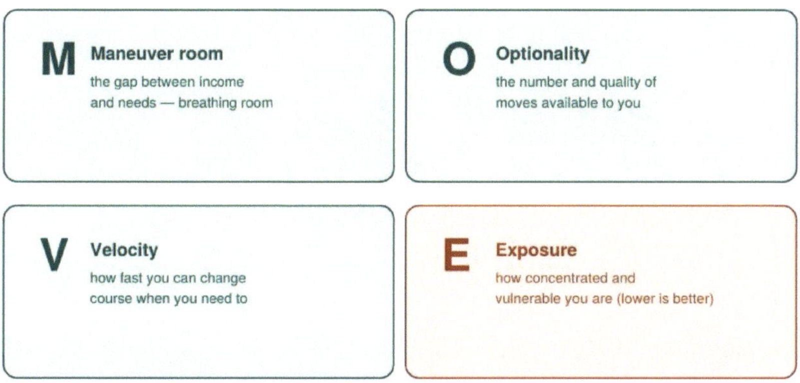

The four dimensions of bend. High maneuver room, optionality, and velocity, paired with low exposure, describe a financial life that can actually move.

The four dimensions

Walk through them. *Maneuver room* is the gap between what you earn and what you need the breathing room from Part Two; without it, nothing else can flex. *Optionality* is the number and quality of moves available to you the cash, skills, and low lock-in from Part Four. *Velocity* is how fast you could actually change course: how quickly you could cut spending, reach cash, or pivot your income if you suddenly had to. And *Exposure* is the mirror image of all of it how concentrated and vulnerable you are: a single income, a heavy fixed-cost base, one illiquid all-in bet. High maneuver room, high optionality, high velocity, low exposure: that is, in four letters, a financial life that can bend.

Scoring yourself

Rate each one honestly a simple one to five is plenty. You're not chasing a perfect score; you're after the *picture*, and especially the weak link. Because flexibility behaves like a chain: it tends to break at its weakest point. It doesn't matter how much maneuver room you have if your velocity is near zero and you can't reach your money when it counts. A balanced, modest profile usually bends better than a lopsided, impressive-looking one.

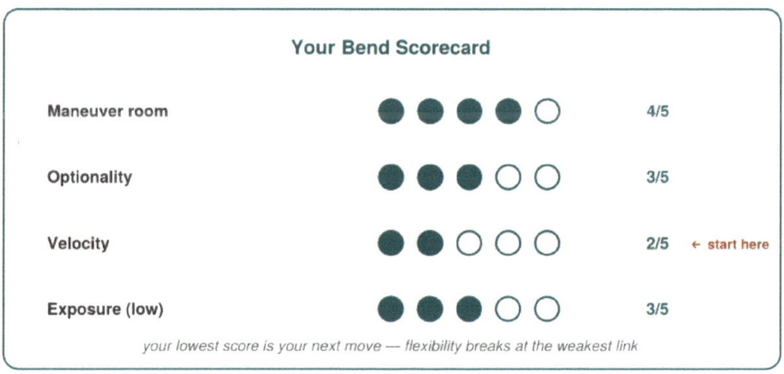

A sample scorecard. The single most useful output isn't the total it's the lowest score, which points straight at where your next effort should go.

That gives you the most useful output of the whole exercise: your lowest score is your next move. Not a vague resolution to "do better with money," but a specific, targeted place to apply effort the velocity you need to build, the exposure you need to reduce where it will do the most good.

A rising score, not a high one

Here's the agile part: you don't do this once. You re-score periodically quarterly is plenty and you watch the trend. The goal on any given day isn't a high score; it's a *rising* one. A financial life getting steadily more flexible is winning, regardless of where it started, and a high score that's quietly slipping is a warning worth catching early.

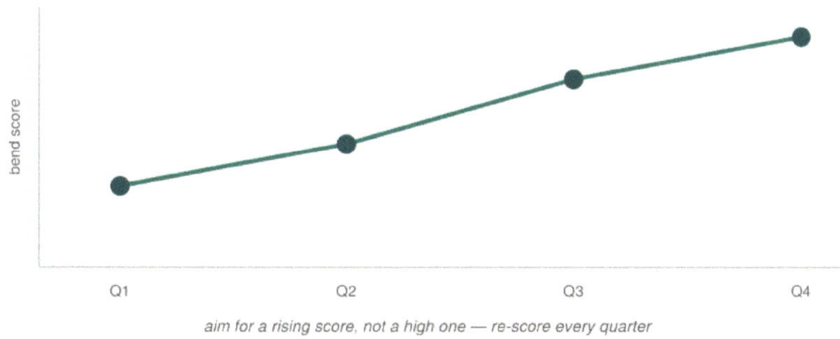

Re-score every quarter and track the trend. A steadily climbing bend score not a perfect one is what tells you the practice is working.

Why measure bend, not just wealth

This quietly reframes the whole project of "doing well with money." The conventional scoreboard rewards accumulation, even the rigid kind the locked-in, high-net-worth life from Chapter 13 scores beautifully on the usual metrics and bends terribly when life moves. The bend scorecard rewards the thing that actually keeps you both safe and free: room to move. Measure that, watch it, and you'll find yourself naturally making the choices this entire book has been pointing toward not out of discipline, but because you can finally see the thing that matters.

Consider Leo, who by every conventional measure was doing well high net worth, high income, an impressive number on the statement. But when he scored his M.O.V.E., the picture changed. His maneuver room was thin (almost everything was reinvested in his business), his velocity was near zero (he couldn't reach most of his wealth quickly), and his exposure was extreme (one business, one industry, one bet). On the old scoreboard he was winning. On the bend scorecard he was dangerously rigid one bad quarter from a crisis despite all that "wealth." Seeing it scored is what finally moved him: he built reachable cash, diversified a slice, and watched his bend score climb even as his net worth held flat. The number he'd been proud of had been measuring the wrong thing.

The scorecard tells you *where* to act. The next chapter is about *how* to actually act how to make change happen instead of merely intending it by borrowing the most practical tool in the whole agile kit: the sprint.

Chapter summary

- Conventional metrics measure the size of your money, not its flexibility; the practice begins by measuring bend.
- M.O.V.E. captures it: Maneuver room (the income-needs gap), Optionality (moves available), Velocity (how fast you can change course), and Exposure (how concentrated and vulnerable you are lower is better).
- Score each dimension honestly; your lowest score is your next move, because flexibility breaks at the weakest link.
- Re-score periodically and aim for a rising score, not a high one a steadily more flexible life is winning wherever it started.

Questions to think about

- Of Maneuver room, Optionality, Velocity, and Exposure, which is your strongest and which is your weakest link?
- How fast, honestly, could you cut your spending or reach cash if you had to? That's your velocity.
- Where are you most dangerously exposed one income, one big, fixed cost, one concentrated bet?
- If you scored yourself today and again in three months, what one change would move the trend up?

Chapter 21 · Timeboxing Your Money

The scorecard told you where to act. But there's a gap between knowing what to do and actually doing it, and most financial good intentions die quietly in that gap. "I should build my buffer." "I should cut my fixed costs." "I should finally learn to invest." All true, all sitting on the mental to-do list for years because a vague, open-ended intention has no force behind it. The agile world has a simple, almost mechanical fix for exactly this problem, and it's the most practical tool in the entire kit: the sprint.

Why open-ended goals don't move

There's a well-known observation called Parkinson's Law: work expands to fill the time available for it. A money goal with no deadline, then, expands to fill the rest of your life which is another way of saying it never actually gets done. "Get better with money" is permanently in progress and permanently unfinished. The problem usually isn't motivation or knowledge; it's structure. An open-ended goal gives your effort nowhere to land and no moment at which it's complete.

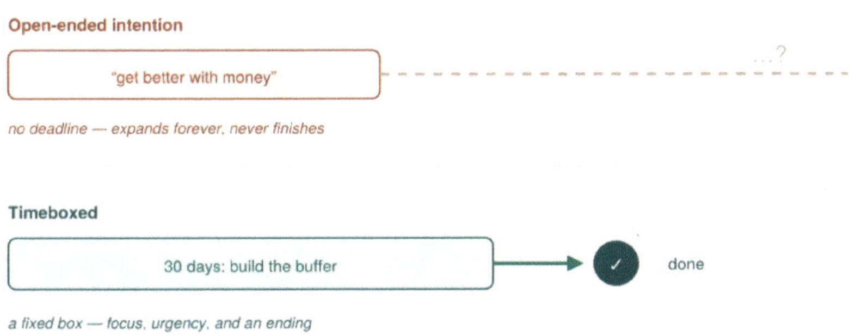

An open-ended intention expands forever and never finishes. A fixed, short box gives the same effort focus, urgency, and crucially an ending.

The timebox

A timebox is the opposite of an open-ended goal: a fixed, short, non-negotiable period assigned to one thing. Not "build the buffer eventually," but "for the next thirty days, the buffer is *the* focus." The power isn't in the time itself; it's in the *boundary*. A deadline creates focus. A short deadline creates urgency. And a fixed one creates an ending a defined moment when you stop, look at what actually happened, and decide what comes next. Things with endings get finished; things without them drift.

The money sprint

Applied to money, this becomes a *money sprint*: pick one focus, give it a fixed short box a month works well and at the end, review and choose the next. One focus, because splitting your attention across five money goals at once is precisely how all five stall. A short box, because that's what creates urgency. And a review at the end, because that's where the learning lives and the next move comes from.

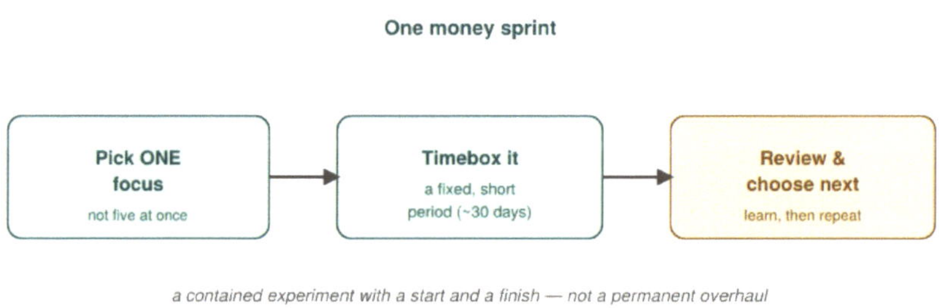

The anatomy of a money sprint: one focus, a fixed short box of time, and a review that turns the experiment into a decision about what to do next.

Notice what a sprint is *not*. It isn't a permanent new rule or a sweeping budget overhaul the kind of thing that's daunting to start and easy to abandon. It's a contained experiment with a clear start and a clear finish. That's exactly what makes it light enough to actually begin, because almost anyone can do one focused thing for a single month, even when "fix my whole financial life" feels impossible.

A year of sprints

String a handful of these together and a year stops being twelve months of vague intentions with no movement, and becomes a series of focused pushes, each building on the last. One month, the buffer. The next, the fixed costs. The next, automating your saving so it happens without you. The next, a skill from Chapter 15. Each individual sprint is small and unintimidating; the compounding across a year is substantial.

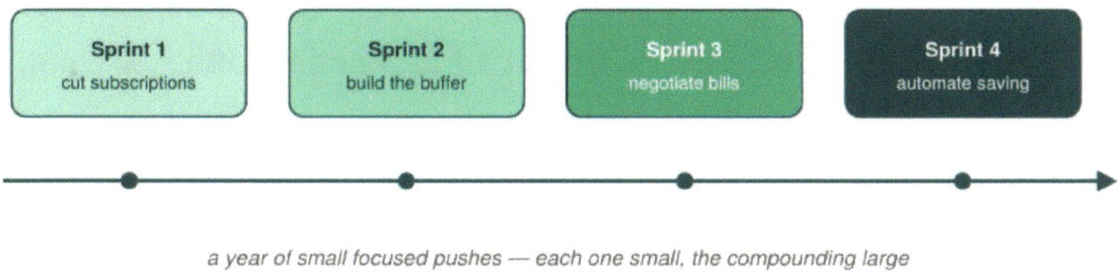

A year as a sequence of small, focused sprints rather than a single overwhelming resolution each one finishable, the results stacking up over time.

And you don't sprint constantly that's a fast road to burnout, and it contradicts the whole spirit of a flexible practice. Plenty of months are simply maintenance, with nothing in particular to push on. You run a sprint when the scorecard from the last chapter shows a weak link that's worth a focused month of attention, and you rest the rest of the time.

Why this beats willpower

The deep reason sprints work is that they don't lean on sustained willpower, which every human being eventually runs out of. They lean on *structure* a small, bounded, finishable commitment. You're not asking yourself to "be disciplined about money forever," which is an exhausting and ultimately impossible request. You're asking for one focused month, and then a rest. That's a request you can actually say yes to and, more importantly, say yes to again and again, which is what builds a flexible life over years.

Consider Carmen, who'd "been meaning to get on top of her spending" for three years a permanent, open-ended intention that never moved. Instead of resolving to be disciplined forever, she ran one 30-day sprint with a single focus: every subscription and recurring charge, reviewed and decided. That was it just thirty days, just that one thing. By the end she'd cancelled seven services she'd forgotten she had and renegotiated two bills, freeing up a meaningful monthly sum and, more importantly, actually finishing something. The next month she rested. The month after, she ran a different sprint. The three-year-old intention had failed because it asked for endless willpower; the sprint succeeded because it asked for one focused month she could actually say yes to.

Sprints make change happen. But to keep getting *better* to genuinely learn from each one rather than just complete it you need a deliberate way to reflect. That's the loop at the very heart of the practice, and it's where we go next.

Chapter summary

- Knowing what to do and doing it are different problems; vague, open-ended money goals stall because they have no boundary and no ending.
- A timebox a fixed, short period assigned to one focus supplies the focus, urgency, and ending that actually get things finished.
- Run money sprints: pick one focus, give it a short fixed box (a month), then review and choose the next; keep them light, contained experiments, not permanent overhauls.
- Sprints beat willpower because they rely on small, bounded, finishable commitments rather than endless discipline; sprint on your weakest link and let plenty of months be maintenance.

Questions to think about

- What money intention has been "in progress" for years with no deadline and what would a 30-day sprint on it look like?
- What's the single focus your scorecard says deserves your next sprint?
- Are you trying to improve five money things at once, and stalling on all five?
- What would make a sprint light enough that you'd actually start it this month?

Chapter 22 · The Reflection Loop

We've been measuring, with the scorecard, and doing, with the sprint. But activity is not the same as improvement. You can run sprint after sprint and still not get any better if you never stop to ask what worked, what didn't, and what to change. The missing piece the engine that turns raw experience into actual improvement is reflection. And reflection works best not as an occasional bout of soul-searching, but as a small, regular loop you barely notice doing.

Plan, Do, Check, Act

The loop comes from the worlds of quality and agile work, and it has four steps. **Plan** a small change. **Do** it try it for real. **Check** honestly what actually happened. **Act** on what you learned: lock in what worked, adjust what didn't. Then plan the next turn. It's called PDCA, and it's deceptively simple simple enough that the crucial step is the one nearly everyone skips. People plan and do endlessly, but they rarely stop to genuinely *check.* The honest looking is not a formality before the next plan; it *is* the point.

And this loop isn't a flat circle spinning in place. Done honestly, each turn leaves you slightly better off than the last a little more flexible, a little wiser about your own patterns. It's less a wheel turning on the spot than a wheel rolling uphill: small, continuous, compounding improvement.

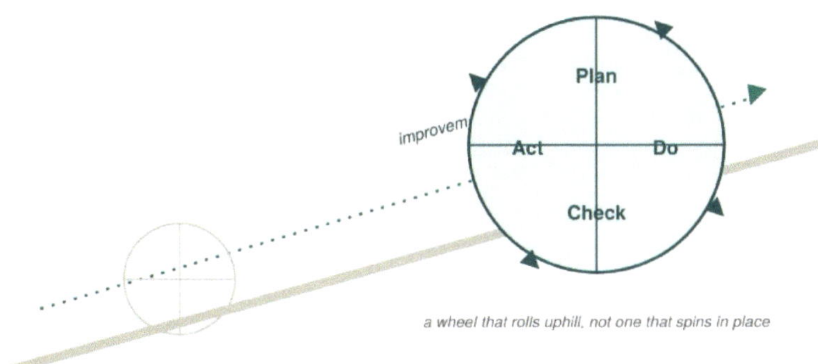

a wheel that rolls uphill, not one that spins in place

The reflection loop, PDCA, drawn as it actually behaves: not a circle spinning in place, but a wheel rolling uphill, each honest turn leaving you a little better than the last.

Two loops for two weathers

You've actually met a loop like this once before the OODA loop back in Chapter 10 and it's worth being precise about the difference, because the two are built for different weather. OODA is the *crisis* cadence: fast, reactive, run over hours and days, designed to help you *survive* a storm. PDCA is the *calm* cadence: slower, reflective, run over weeks and months, designed to help you *grow* when nothing is on fire. You need both and you need to know which one you're in. Running OODA when you should be calmly reflecting keeps you twitchy and short-term; running PDCA when the house is burning is far too slow.

Two cadences for two kinds of weather. PDCA is the slow, reflective loop for improving in calm; OODA is the fast, reactive loop for surviving a storm.

A rhythm, not an event

The trick to actually keeping a reflection loop is to make it a light rhythm at several scales, so it never balloons into a dreaded annual reckoning. A two-minute glance each week am I on track? A fifteen-minute review at the end of each monthly sprint what did I learn? A thirty-minute quarterly re-score of the bend scorecard. And once a year, an hour with the manifesto and the long vision are these still right? Each cadence sits nested inside the larger one, and small-and-regular beats big-and-rare here exactly as it has everywhere else in this book.

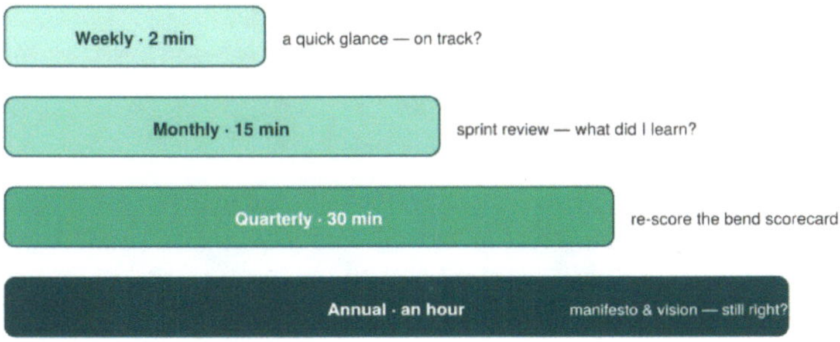

Reflection as a set of nested rhythms a quick weekly glance inside a monthly review inside a quarterly re-score inside an annual look at your values so it stays light and never becomes a dreaded event.

The circle of self-growth

There's a quiet psychological shift hiding inside all of this. When reflection becomes a regular, structured loop, mistakes stop being *verdicts* and start being *data* simply inputs to the next turn of the wheel. This is the blameless retro from Chapter 11, made into a habit: you're no longer sitting in judgment of yourself, you're running experiments and reading the results. That reframe from judgment to iteration is what transforms reflection from something faintly painful into something genuinely growthful. It becomes a circle of self-growth rather than a cycle of self-criticism, and that is the difference between a practice you keep and one you quietly abandon.

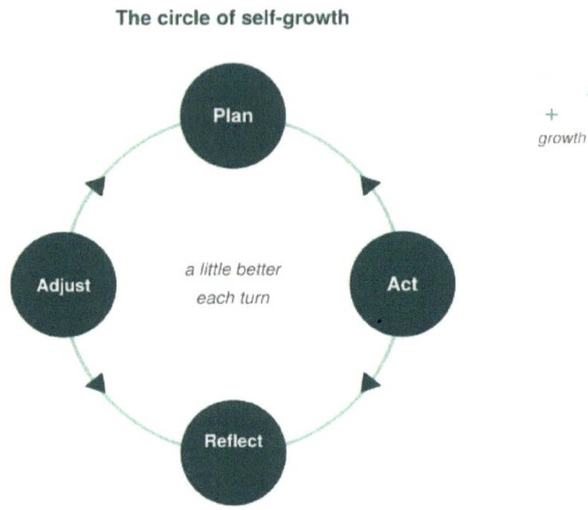

The circle of self-growth plan, act, reflect, adjust, then round again, each honest turn leaving you a little better than the last.

Consider Ravindra, who set a standing fifteen minutes on the first of each month to run a simple loop on his money: what did I plan, what actually happened, what did I learn, what will I change? At first it felt clumsy and faintly pointless. But over a year the small turns compounded. One month he noticed a creeping subscription; the next, he caught that his "emergency" buffer was quietly being raided for non-emergencies; the next, he adjusted a savings transfer that no longer fit. None of these were dramatic. But each was a tiny correction he'd have missed without the loop, and together they bent his trajectory meaningfully upward. He wasn't more disciplined than anyone else. He'd just built a small, regular circle that turned ordinary mistakes into steady self-correction.

But a loop needs someone to run it honestly, kindly, and persistently, week after week. That someone is you, in a role most people never consciously step into: your own coach. That's the next chapter.

Chapter summary

- Activity isn't improvement; running sprints without reflection won't make you better reflection is the engine that turns experience into improvement.

- The PDCA loop Plan, Do, Check, Act is the reflective cadence; the step people skip is Check, and the loop climbs: each honest turn leaves you a little better.
- PDCA is the calm-weather cadence for improving over weeks and months; OODA is the storm cadence for surviving in hours and days you need both, matched to the weather.
- Make reflection a light rhythm at several nested scales; structured reflection turns mistakes from verdicts into data a circle of self-growth rather than self-criticism.

Questions to think about

- After your last money decision or sprint, did you ever actually "Check" honestly look at what happened?
- Are you running the right loop for your weather reflecting in calm, acting fast in a crisis?
- What would a two-minute weekly and a fifteen-minute monthly money reflection look like for you?
- Where are you treating a money mistake as a verdict about yourself instead of data for the next turn?

Chapter 23 · Coach Yourself Forward

The reflection loop needs a driver someone to actually run it, week after week, honestly and persistently. For your financial life, that someone is you. But here's what most people miss: you don't run it as a neutral observer. You run it as one of two characters, and which one you choose changes everything. You can be your own harshest critic, or your own best coach. Same person, same facts, radically different results.

The critic and the coach

When something goes wrong with money, two inner voices are always available. There's the *critic:* "you always do this, you're hopeless with money, why even try." It feels like accountability, but it's really just the shame from Chapters 11 and 12 wearing a stern face, and it reliably produces avoidance and paralysis. And there's the *coach:* "okay, what happened? What can you learn? What's one thing you'll try next?" It holds you to a real standard, but without contempt. The critic asks *what's wrong with you;* the coach asks *what will you do.* Only one of those questions has an answer you can actually act on.

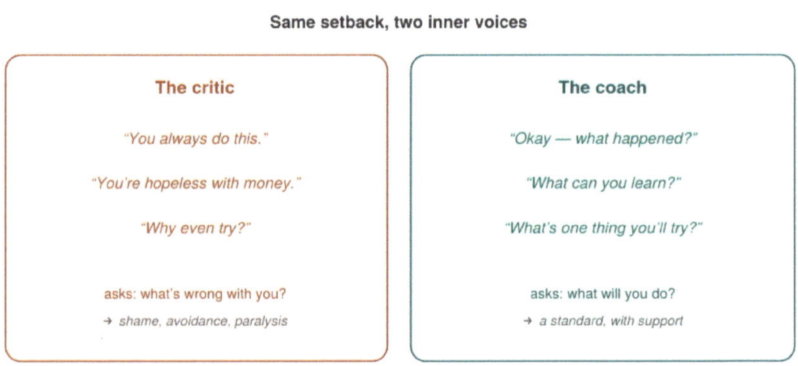

The same setback meets two inner voices. The critic asks what's wrong with you and produces hiding; the coach asks what you'll do and produces a next step.

This is emphatically not about going easy on yourself. A good coach is *demanding* they expect real effort and don't accept excuses but they are unmistakably on your side. That specific combination, high standards paired with genuine support, is what actually changes behavior over time. Contempt, however rigorous it feels, just teaches you to hide from your own finances.

Ask better questions

In practice, coaching is mostly the discipline of asking better questions than the critic does. One simple, well-worn structure is the GROW model: **Goal** (what do I actually want here?), **Reality** (what's honestly true right now?), **Options** (what could I do?), and **Will** (what will I commit to, and by when?). Run a vague money worry through those four questions and it turns into a concrete next step and notice that every one of them faces forward. The critic relitigates the past; the coach builds the next move.

The GROW questions turn a vague money worry into a concrete next step goal, then honest reality, then options, then a real commitment.

Borrow accountability when you need it

Self-coaching is powerful, but it has one well-known weakness: it's easy to quietly let yourself off the hook when no one else is watching. The fix is to borrow accountability from outside whenever your own isn't enough and there's a whole spectrum to draw on, from a private written commitment, to telling a friend, to a regular check-in with a partner, all the way to a paid coach or advisor. The rule is simple: reach further out the more your internal discipline is failing on a given goal.

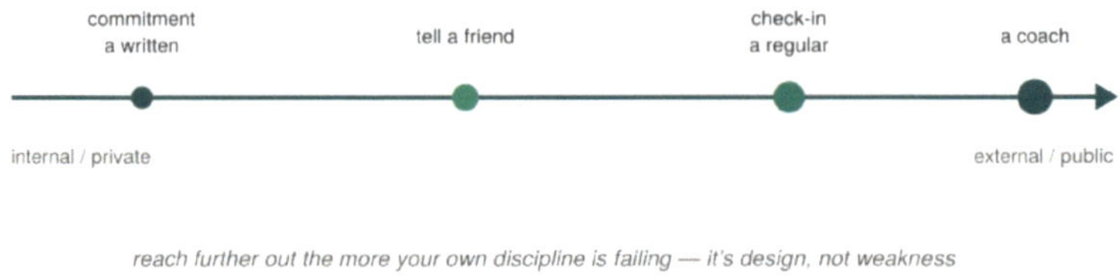

A spectrum of accountability, from a private written commitment to an outside coach. Reach further toward the external end the more your own discipline is coming up short.

And needing that external structure is not a weakness it's good design. You already use it everywhere else without shame: deadlines, trainers, teammates, due dates. Building the same scaffolding around your money is just engineering your environment so the right thing is more likely to happen, which is exactly what a good coach helps you do.

Be the coach you'd want

The deepest version of all this is simply to talk to yourself about money the way a great coach would honestly, demandingly, and unmistakably on your side. It can sound soft, but it's the opposite. The critic's contempt feels rigorous and produces stagnation; the coach's steady, high-standards support produces the one thing that actually matters over a lifetime, which is that you keep going. Because the people who do best with money across decades are almost never the ones who never stumble. They're the ones who coach themselves back up, again and again, without the detour through self-contempt.

Consider Grace again, facing a money decision that had gone badly an investment that dropped right after she bought in. Her first inner voice was the critic: *you always do this, you're hopeless, why do you even try.* She caught it, and deliberately switched voices. The coach asked different questions: *okay what actually happened here? What can you learn? What's one thing you'll do differently next time?* Same facts, same loss. But the critic's version left her too ashamed to even look at her accounts for weeks, which only made things worse. The coach's version had her calmly adjust her approach and keep going. She wasn't going easy on herself the coach still held a high standard. It was simply on her side, and that was the whole difference between hiding and improving.

And with that, the practice is complete: measure, sprint, reflect, coach. All that remains is to put it together and to step back and see the whole life you've been learning to build. That's the final chapter.

Chapter summary

- Every reflection loop needs a driver; for your money that's you and you run it either as your own harshest critic or your own best coach, with very different results.
- The critic ("what's wrong with you?") is shame in disguise and produces avoidance; the coach ("what will you do?") holds high standards with genuine support and produces action.
- Coaching is mostly better questions: the GROW model Goal, Reality, Options, Will turns a vague money worry into a concrete, forward-looking next step.
- Borrow external accountability (a written commitment, a friend, a partner, a coach) when self-discipline runs low; that's good design, not weakness.

Questions to think about

- When something goes wrong with money, which voice do you default to the critic or the coach?
- Take a current money worry through GROW: what's the goal, the reality, your options, and what will you commit to?
- Where would a little external accountability make you far more likely to follow through?
- What would it sound like to talk to yourself about money the way a great coach would?

Chapter 24 · Build a Life That Can Bend

We began with a promise that no longer holds: the straight line. Study, work, save, retire a clean path through a predictable world. The trouble, as this whole book has argued, is that the world stopped being predictable, and a financial life built for a straight line cracks the moment the line bends. Everything since has been about building the alternative not a life that resists change, but one that moves with it. A life that's built to bend.

What we built

Step back and look at the whole shape of it. It rests on a foundation of values your manifesto, the thing that decides for you when you're under pressure. On that foundation stand three capacities: the ability to *adapt* in ordinary weather, to *protect* against storms, and to *grow* by widening your options. Those three carry you through every major transition a life can bring. And a light, repeating practice measure, sprint, reflect, coach keeps the whole structure alive and adjusting, instead of quietly hardening back into rigidity over the years.

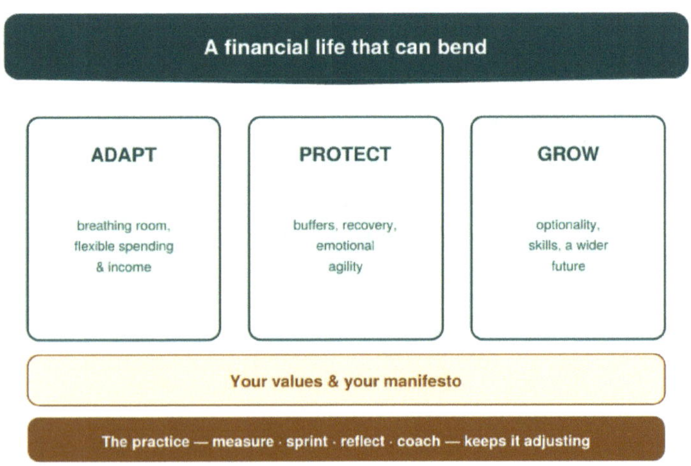

The whole structure: values underneath, the capacity to adapt, protect, and grow above, and a light practice running through it all to keep it bending rather than setting.

And notice what none of it required. It didn't depend on being rich, on predicting the future, or on never making a mistake. It depended only on building room to move and on the practice to keep that room open over time. Those are available to almost anyone, at almost any income, starting from almost anywhere.

From rigid to bendable

The journey, put as plainly as possible, is a move from one kind of financial life to another. From a single income to several streams. From no cushion to real breathing room. From maxed-out and locked-in to buffered and optioned. From reacting in fear to responding from values. From a structure that looks impressive right up until the moment it's tested, to one that may look more modest but quietly holds.

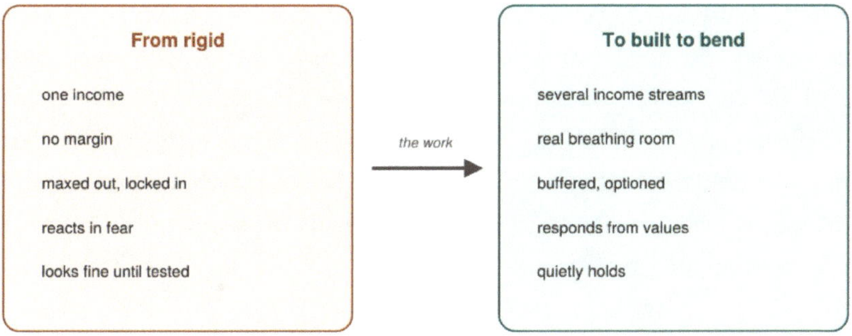

The arc of the whole book: the same life, moved from rigid to bendable not necessarily richer, but far harder to break.

It was never really about money

Here is the thing this book has been about underneath the money the entire time. Flexibility isn't a financial tactic; it's a way of meeting an uncertain world without being ruled by the fear of it. The breathing room, the options, the buffers their deepest payoff was never financial. It's the freedom to choose your life on your own terms: to say yes to what matters and no to what doesn't, to take a real chance, to absorb a loss, to change your mind, to walk a path that isn't straight. Money that can bend buys something far larger than money. It buys a life you actually get to steer.

Start small, start now

You don't have to do all of it, and you certainly don't have to do any of it perfectly. Pick the single place your money is most rigid the weakest link on your scorecard and run one small sprint at it this month. Then reflect on what happened. Then the next. Flexibility, like everything that genuinely lasts, is built one small, repeatable move at a time. The goal was never a perfect financial life; there's no such thing, and chasing it is its own kind of rigidity. The goal was a life that can bend without breaking and you can begin building it today, exactly where you are.

Consider Marcus once more the freelancer from early in this book, who used to scramble every time a client paid late. He didn't transform his finances in a weekend. He picked the single weakest link his nonexistent buffer and ran one small sprint at it. Then he reflected, and picked the next: steadier income streams. Then the next: low, flexible fixed costs. None of it was heroic, and none of it was fast. But a few years of small, repeatable moves turned a fragile financial life into one that bends. The late-paying client that once meant panic is now barely a blip. He never became rich, or certain about the future. He just became hard to break which, it turns out, was the thing he'd actually wanted all along.

A straight line snaps under pressure. A life that's built to bend just keeps going.

Chapter summary

- A financial life built for a straight-line cracks when the line bends; the alternative is one that moves with change built to bend.
- The whole structure rests on values, stands on the capacity to adapt, protect, and grow, carries you through transitions, and is kept alive by a light practice of measure, sprint, reflect, and coach.
- None of it requires being rich, predicting the future, or never erring only building room to move and keeping it open; the deepest payoff is the freedom to steer your own life.
- You don't have to do it all or perfectly; pick the weakest link, run one small sprint this month, reflect, and repeat flexibility is built one small move at a time.

Questions to think about

- Looking back across the book, where is your financial life most rigid right now and what's the one weakest link to start with?
- What's the single small sprint you could begin this month?
- Beyond money, what would more room to move actually let you do, or say yes to, or stop fearing?
- A year from now, what would tell you your financial life had become more able to bend?

www.ingramcontent.com/pod-product-compliance
Lightning Source LLC
LaVergne TN
LVHW051135210926
848482LV00006B/319